PENGUIN BOOKS — GREAT IDEAS

When I Dare To Be Powerful

Audre Lorde
1934–1992

Audre Lorde

When I Dare to be Powerful

PENGUIN BOOKS — GREAT IDEAS

PENGUIN BOOKS

UK | USA | Canada | Ireland | Australia
India | New Zealand | South Africa

Penguin Books is part of the Penguin Random House group
of companies whose addresses can be found at
global.penguinrandomhouse.com.

Penguin
Random House
UK

Essays first published in *Sister Outsider* 1984
This selection published in Penguin Books 2020
006

Set in 12/15 pt Dante MT Std
Typeset by Jouve (UK), Milton Keynes
Printed and bound in Great Britain by Clays Ltd, Elcograf S.p.A.

A CIP catalogue record for this book
is available from the British Library

ISBN: 978-0-241-47315-3

www.greenpenguin.co.uk

MIX
Paper | Supporting
responsible forestry
FSC® C018179

Penguin Random House is committed to a
sustainable future for our business, our readers
and our planet. This book is made from Forest
Stewardship Council® certified paper.

Contents

Contents

The Transformation of Silence into Language and Action[1]

I have come to believe over and over again that what is most important to me must be spoken, made verbal and shared, even at the risk of having it bruised or misunderstood. That the speaking profits me, beyond any other effect. I am standing here as a Black lesbian poet, and the meaning of all that waits upon the fact that I am still alive, and might not have been. Less than two months ago I was told by two doctors, one female and one male, that I would have to have breast surgery, and that there was a 60 to 80 percent chance that the tumor was malignant. Between that telling and the actual surgery, there was a three-week period of the agony of an

1. Paper delivered at the Modern Language Association's 'Lesbian and Literature Panel,' Chicago, Illinois, December 28, 1977. First published in *Sinister Wisdom* 6 (1978) and The *Cancer Journals* (Spinsters, Ink, San Francisco, 1980).

involuntary reorganization of my entire life. The surgery was completed, and the growth was benign.

But within those three weeks, I was forced to look upon myself and my living with a harsh and urgent clarity that has left me still shaken but much stronger. This is a situation faced by many women, by some of you here today. Some of what I experienced during that time has helped elucidate for me much of what I feel concerning the transformation of silence into language and action.

In becoming forcibly and essentially aware of my mortality, and of what I wished and wanted for my life, however short it might be, priorities and omissions became strongly etched in a merciless light, and what I most regretted were my silences. Of what had I ever been afraid? To question or to speak as I believed could have meant pain, or death. But we all hurt in so many different ways, all the time, and pain will either change or end. Death, on the other hand, is the final silence. And that might be coming quickly, now, without regard for whether I had ever spoken what needed to be said, or had only betrayed myself into small silences, while I planned someday to speak, or waited for someone else's words. And I began to recognize a source of power within myself that comes from the knowledge that while it is most desirable not to be afraid, learning to put fear into a perspective gave me great strength.

I was going to die, if not sooner then later, whether or not I had ever spoken myself. My silences had not protected me. Your silence will not protect you. But for every real word spoken, for every attempt I had ever made to speak those truths for which I am still seeking, I had made contact with other women while we examined the words to fit a world in which we all believed, bridging our differences. And it was the concern and caring of all those women which gave me strength and enabled me to scrutinize the essentials of my living.

The women who sustained me through that period were Black and white, old and young, lesbian, bisexual, and heterosexual, and we all shared a war against the tyrannies of silence. They all gave me a strength and concern without which I could not have survived intact. Within those weeks of acute fear came the knowledge – within the war we are all waging with the forces of death, subtle and otherwise, conscious or not – I am not only a casualty, I am also a warrior.

What are the words you do not yet have? What do you need to say? What are the tyrannies you swallow day by day and attempt to make your own, until you will sicken and die of them, still in silence?

Perhaps for some of you here today, I am the face of one of your fears. Because I am woman, because I am Black, because I am lesbian, because I am myself – a Black woman warrior poet doing my work – come to ask you, are you doing yours?

And of course I am afraid, because the transformation of silence into language and action is an act of self-revelation, and that always seems fraught with danger. But my daughter, when I told her of our topic and my difficulty with it, said, 'Tell them about how you're never really a whole person if you remain silent, because there's always that one little piece inside you that wants to be spoken out, and if you keep ignoring it, it gets madder and hotter and hotter, and if you don't speak it out one day it will just up and punch you in the mouth from the inside.'

In the cause of silence, each of us draws the face of her own fear – fear of contempt, of censure, or some judgment, or recognition, of challenge, of annihilation. But most of all, I think, we fear the visibility without which we cannot truly live. Within this country where racial difference creates a constant, if unspoken, distortion of vision, Black women have on one hand always been highly visible, and so, on the other hand, have been rendered invisible through the depersonalization of racism. Even within the women's movement, we have had to fight, and still do, for that very visibility which also renders us most vulnerable, our Blackness. For to survive in the mouth of this dragon we call america, we have had to learn this first and most vital lesson – that we were never meant to survive. Not as human beings. And neither were most of you here today, Black or not. And that visibility which makes us most vulnerable is that which also is the source of our greatest strength. Because the machine will try to grind you into dust anyway, whether or not we speak. We can sit in our corners mute forever while our sisters and our selves are wasted, while our children are distorted and destroyed, while our earth is poisoned; we can sit in our safe corners mute as bottles, and we will still be no less afraid.

In my house this year we are celebrating the feast of Kwanza, the African–american festival of harvest which begins the day after Christmas and lasts for seven days. There are seven principles of Kwanza, one for each day. The first principle is Umoja, which means unity, the decision to strive for and maintain unity in self and community. The principle for yesterday, the second day, was Kujichagulia – self-determination – the decision to define ourselves, name ourselves, and speak for ourselves, instead of being defined and spoken for by others. Today is the third day of Kwanza, and the principle for today is Ujima – collective work and responsibility – the decision to build and maintain ourselves and our communities together and to recognize and solve our problems together.

Each of us is here now because in one way or another we share a commitment to language and to the power of language, and to the reclaiming of that language which has been made to work against us. In the transformation of silence into language and action, it is vitally necessary for each one of us to establish or examine her function in that transformation and to recognize her role as vital within that transformation.

For those of us who write, it is necessary to scrutinize not only the truth of what we speak, but the truth of that language by which we speak it. For others, it is to share and spread also those words that are meaningful to us. But primarily for us all, it is necessary to teach by living and speaking those truths which we believe and know beyond understanding. Because in this way alone we can survive, by taking part in a process of life that is creative and continuing, that is growth.

And it is never without fear – of visibility, of the harsh light of scrutiny and perhaps judgment, of pain, of death. But we have lived through all of those already, in silence, except death. And I remind myself all the time now that if I were to have been born mute, or had maintained an oath of silence my whole life long for safety, I would still have suffered, and I would still die. It is very good for establishing perspective.

And where the words of women are crying to be heard, we must each of us recognize our responsibility to seek those words out, to read them and share them and examine them in their pertinence to our lives. That we not hide behind the mockeries of separations that have been imposed upon us and which so often we accept as our own. For instance, 'I can't possibly teach Black women's writing – their experience is so different from mine.' Yet how many years have you spent teaching Plato and Shakespeare and Proust? Or another, 'She's a white woman and what could she possibly have to say to me?' Or, 'She's a lesbian, what would my husband say, or my chairman?' Or again, 'This woman writes of her sons and I have no children.' And all the other endless ways in which we rob ourselves of ourselves and each other.

We can learn to work and speak when we are afraid in the same way we have learned to work and speak when we are tired. For we have been socialized to respect fear more than our own needs for language and definition, and while we wait in silence for that final luxury of fearlessness, the weight of that silence will choke us.

The fact that we are here and that I speak these words is an attempt to break that silence and bridge some of those differences between us, for it is not difference which immobilizes us, but silence. And there are so many silences to be broken.

An Open Letter to Mary Daly

The following letter was written to Mary Daly, author of Gyn/Ecology[1] *on May 6, 1979. Four months later, having received no reply, I open it to the community of women.*

Dear Mary,

With a moment of space in this wild and bloody spring,[2] I want to speak the words I have had in mind for you. I had hoped that our paths might cross and we could sit down together and talk, but this has not happened.

I wish you strength and satisfaction in your eventual victory over the repressive forces of the University in Boston. I am glad so many women attended the speak-out, and hope that this show

1. *Gyn/Ecology: The Metaethics of Radical Feminism* (Beacon Press, Bositon, 1978).

2. In the spring of 1979, twelve Black women were murdered in the Boston area.

of joined power will make more space for you to grow and be within.

Thank you for having *Gyn/Ecology* sent to me. So much of it is full of import, useful, generative, and provoking. As in *Beyond God The Father*, many of your analyses are strengthening and helpful to me. Therefore, it is because of what you have given to me in the past work that I write this letter to you now, hoping to share with you the benefits of my insights as you have shared the benefits of yours with me.

This letter has been delayed because of my grave reluctance to reach out to you, for what I want us to chew upon here is neither easy nor simple. The history of white women who are unable to hear Black women's words, or to maintain dialogue with us, is long and discouraging. But for me to assume that you will not hear me represents not only history, perhaps, but an old pattern of relating, sometimes protective and sometimes dysfunctional, which we, as women shaping our future, are in the process of shattering and passing beyond, I hope.

I believe in your good faith toward all women, in your vision of a future within which we can all flourish, and in your commitment to the hard and often painful work necessary to effect change. In this spirit I invite you to a joint clarification of some of the differences which lie between us as a Black and a white woman.

When I started reading *Gyn/Ecology*, I was truly excited by the vision behind your words and nodded my head as you spoke in your First Passage of myth and mystification. Your words on the nature and function of the Goddess, as well as the ways in which her face has been obscured, agreed with what I myself have discovered in my searches through African myth/legend/religion for the true nature of old female power.

So I wondered, why doesn't Mary deal with Afrekete as an example? Why are her goddess images only white, western european, judeochristian? Where was Afrekete, Yemanje, Oyo, and Mawulisa? Where were the warrior goddesses of the Vodun, the Dahomeian Amazons and the warrior-women of Dan? Well, I thought, Mary has made a conscious decision to narrow her scope and to deal only with the ecology of western european women.

Then I came to the first three chapters of your Second Passage, and it was obvious that you were dealing with noneuropean women, but only as victims and preyers-upon each other. I began to feel my history and my mythic background distorted by the absence of any images of my foremothers in power. Your inclusion of African genital mutilation was an important and necessary piece in any consideration of female ecology, and too little has been written about it. To imply, however, that all women suffer the same oppression simply because we are women is to lose sight of the many varied tools of patriarchy. It is to ignore how those tools are used by women without awareness against each other.

To dismiss our Black foremothers may well be to dismiss where european women learned to love. As an African-american woman in white patriarchy, I am used to having my archetypal experience distorted and trivialized, but it is terribly painful to feel it being done by a woman whose knowledge so much touches my own.

When I speak of knowledge, as you know, I am speaking of that dark and true depth which understanding serves, waits upon, and makes accessible through language to ourselves and others. It is this depth within each of us that nurtures vision.

What you excluded from *Gyn/Ecology* dismissed my heritage and the heritage of all other noneuropean women, and denied the real connections that exist between all of us.

It is obvious that you have done a tremendous amount of work for this book. But simply because so little material on non-white female power and symbol exists in white women's words from a radical feminist perspective, to exclude this aspect of connection from even comment in your work is to deny the fountain of noneuropean female strength and power that nurtures each of our visions. It is to make a point by choice.

Then, to realize that the only quotations from Black women's words were the ones you used to introduce your chapter on African genital mutilation made me question why you needed to use them at all. For my part, I felt that you had in fact misused my words, utilized them only to testify against myself as a woman of Color. For my words which you used were no more, nor less, illustrative of this chapter than 'Poetry is Not a Luxury' or any number of any other poems might have been of many other parts of *Gyn/Ecology*.

So the question arises in my mind, Mary, do you ever really read the work of Black women? Did you ever read my words, or did you merely finger through them for quotations which you thought might valuably support an already conceived idea concerning some old and distorted connection between us? This is not a rhetorical question.

To me, this feels like another instance of the knowledge, croneology and work of women of

Color being ghettoized by a white woman dealing only out of a patriarchal western european frame of reference. Even your words on page 49 of *Gyn/Ecology*, 'The strength which Self-centering women find, in finding our Background, is our *own* strength, which we give back to our Selves,' have a different ring as we remember the old traditions of power and strength and nurturance found in the female bonding of African women. It is there to be tapped by all women who do not fear the revelation of connection to themselves.

Have you read my work, and the work of other Black women, for what it could give you? Or did you hunt through only to find words that would legitimize your chapter on African genital mutilation in the eyes of other Black women? And if so, then why not use our words to legitimize or illustrate the other places where we connect in our being and becoming? If, on the other hand, it was not Black women you were attempting to reach, in what way did our words illustrate your point for white women?

Mary, I ask that you be aware of how this serves the destructive forces of racism and separation between women – the assumption that the herstory and myth of white women is the legitimate and sole herstory and myth of all women to call upon for power and background, and that non-white women and our herstories are noteworthy only as decorations, or examples of female victimization. I ask that you be aware of the effect that this dismissal has upon the community of Black women and other women of Color, and how it devalues your own words. This dismissal does not essentially differ from the specialized devaluations that make Black women prey, for instance, to the murders even now happening in your own city. When patriarchy dismisses us, it encourages our murderers. When radical lesbian feminist theory dismisses us, it encourages its own demise.

This dismissal stands as a real block to communication between us. This block makes it far easier to turn away from you completely than to attempt to understand the thinking behind your choices. Should the next step be war between us, or separation? Assimilation within a solely western european herstory is not acceptable.

Mary, I ask that you re-member what is dark and ancient and divine within yourself that aids your speaking. As outsiders, we need each other for support and connection and all the other necessities of living on the borders. But in order to come together we must recognize each other. Yet I feel that since you have so completely un-recognized me, perhaps I have been in error concerning you and no longer recognize you.

I feel you do celebrate differences between white women as a creative force toward change, rather than a reason for misunderstanding and separation. But you fail to recognize that, as women, those differences expose all women to various forms and degrees of patriarchal oppression, some of which we share and some of which we do not. For instance, surely you know that for nonwhite women in this country, there is an 80 percent fatality rate from breast cancer, three times the number of unnecessary eventrations, hysterectomies and sterilizations as for white women: three times as many chances of being raped, murdered, or assaulted as exist for white women. These are statistical facts, not coincidences nor paranoid fantasies.

Within the community of women, racism is a reality force in my life as it is not in yours. The white women with hoods on in Ohio handing out KKK literature on the street may not like what you have to say, but they will shoot me on sight. (If you and I were to walk into a classroom of women in Dismal Gulch, Alabama, where the only thing they knew about each of us was that we were both Lesbian/Radical/Feminist, you would see exactly what I mean.)

An Open Letter to Mary Daly

The oppression of women knows no ethnic nor racial boundaries, true, but that does not mean it is identical within those differences. Nor do the reservoirs of our ancient power know these boundaries. To deal with one without even alluding to the other is to distort our commonality as well as our difference.

For then beyond sisterhood is still racism.

We first met at the MLA panel, 'The Transformation of Silence Into Language and Action.' This letter attempts to break a silence which I had imposed upon myself shortly before that date. I had decided never again to speak to white women about racism. I felt it was wasted energy because of destructive guilt and defensiveness, and because whatever I had to say might better be said by white women to one another at far less emotional cost to the speaker, and probably with a better hearing. But I would like not to destroy you in my consciousness, not to have to. So as a sister Hag, I ask you to speak to my perceptions.

Whether or not you do, Mary, again I thank you for what I have learned from you.

This letter is in repayment.

In the hands of Afrekete.
Audre Lorde

Eye to Eye: Black Women, Hatred, and Anger[1]

Where does the pain go when it goes away?[2]

Every Black woman in america lives her life somewhere along a wide curve of ancient and unexpressed angers.

My Black woman's anger is a molten pond at the core of me, my most fiercely guarded secret. I know how much of my life as a powerful feeling woman is laced through with this net of rage. It is an electric

1. An abbreviated version of this essay was published in *Essence,* vol. 14, no. 6 (October 1983). I wish to thank the following women without whose insights and support I could not have completed this paper: Andrea Canaan, Frances Clayton, Michelle Cliff, Blanche Wiesen Cook, Clare Coss, Yvonne Flowers, Gloria Joseph, Adrienne Rich, Charlotte Sheedy, Judy Simmons and Barbara Smith. This paper is dedicated to the memory of Sheila Blackwell Pinckney, 1953–1983.

2. From a poem by Dr Gloria Joseph.

thread woven into every emotional tapestry upon which I set the essentials of my life – a boiling hot spring likely to erupt at any point, leaping out of my consciousness like a fire on the landscape. How to train that anger with accuracy rather than deny it has been one of the major tasks of my life.

Other Black women are not the root cause nor the source of that pool of anger. I know this, no matter what the particular situation may be between me and another Black woman at the moment. Then why does that anger unleash itself most tellingly against another Black woman at the least excuse? Why do I judge her in a more critical light than any other, becoming enraged when she does not measure up?

And if behind the object of my attack should lie the face of my own self, unaccepted, then what could possibly quench a fire fueled by such reciprocating passions?

When I started to write about the intensity of the angers between Black women, I found I had only begun to touch one tip of a three-pronged iceberg, the deepest understructure of which was Hatred, that societal deathwish directed against us from the moment we were born Black and female in america. From that moment on we have been steeped in hatred – for our color, for our sex, for our effrontery in daring to presume we had any right to live. As children we absorbed that hatred, passed it through ourselves, and for the most part, we still live our lives outside of the recognition of what that hatred really is and how it functions. Echoes of it return as cruelty and anger in our dealings with each other. For each of us bears the face that hatred seeks, and we have each learned to be at home with cruelty because we have survived so much of it within our own lives.

Before I can write about Black women's anger, I must write about the poisonous seepage of hatred that fuels that anger, and of the cruelty that is spawned when they meet.

I have found this out by scrutinizing my own expectations of other Black women, by following the threads of my own rage at Blackwomanness back into the hatred and despisal that embroidered my life with fire long before I knew where that hatred came from, or why it was being heaped upon me. Children know only themselves as reasons for the happenings in their lives. So of course as a child I decided there must be something terribly wrong with me that inspired such contempt. The bus driver didn't look at other people like that. All the things my mother had warned me not to do and be that I had gone right ahead and done and been must be to blame.

To search for power within myself means I must be willing to move through being afraid to whatever lies beyond. If I look at my most vulnerable places and acknowledge the pain I have felt, I can remove the source of that pain from my enemies' arsenals. My history cannot be used to feather my enemies' arrows then, and that lessens their power over me. Nothing I accept about myself can be used against me to diminish me. I am who I am, doing what I came to do, acting upon you like a drug or a chisel to remind you of your me-ness, as I discover you in myself.

America's measurement of me has lain like a barrier across the realization of my own powers. It was a barrier which I had to examine and dismantle, piece by painful piece, in order to use my energies fully and creatively. It is easier to deal with the external manifestations of racism and sexism than it is to deal with the results of those distortions internalized within our consciousness of ourselves and one another.

But what is the nature of that reluctance to connect with each other on any but the most superficial levels? What is the source of that mistrust and distance maintained between Black women?

*

I don't like to talk about hate. I don't like to remember the cancellation and hatred, heavy as my wished-for death, seen in the eyes of so many white people from the time I could see. It was echoed in newspapers and movies and holy pictures and comic books and *Amos 'n Andy* radio programs. I had no tools to dissect it, no language to name it.

The AA subway train to Harlem. I clutch my mother's sleeve, her arms full of shopping bags, christmas-heavy. The wet smell of winter clothes, the train's lurching. My mother spots an almost seat, pushes my little snowsuited body down. On one side of me a man reading a paper. On the other, a woman in a fur hat staring at me. Her mouth twitches as she stares and then her gaze drops down, pulling mine with it. Her leather-gloved hand plucks at the line where my new blue snowpants and her sleek fur coat meet. She jerks her coat closer to her. I look. I do not see whatever terrible thing she is seeing on the seat between us – probably a roach. But she has communicated her horror to me. It must be something very bad from the way she's looking, so I pull my snowsuit closer to me away from it, too. When I look up the woman is still staring at me, her nose holes and eyes huge. And suddenly I realize there is nothing crawling up the seat between us; it is me she doesn't want her coat to touch. The fur brushes past my face as she stands with a shudder and holds on to a strap in the speeding train. Born and bred a New York City child, I quickly slide over to make room for my mother to sit down. No word has been spoken. I'm afraid to say anything to my mother because I don't know what I've done. I look at the sides of my snowpants, secretly. Is there something on them? Something's going on here I do not understand, but I will never forget it. Her eyes. The flared nostrils. The hate.

My three-year-old eyes ache from the machinery used to test them. My forehead is sore. I have been poked and prodded in the eyes and stared into all morning. I huddle into the tall metal and leather chair, frightened and miserable and wanting my mother. On the other side of the eye clinic's examining room, a group of young white men in white coats discuss my peculiar eyes. Only one voice remains in my memory. 'From the looks of her she's probably simple, too.' They all laugh. One of them comes over to me, enunciating slowly and carefully, 'OK, girlie, go wait outside now.' He pats me on the cheek. I am grateful for the absence of harshness.

The Story Hour librarian reading *Little Black Sambo*. Her white fingers hold up the little book about a shoebutton-faced little boy with big red lips and many pigtails and a hatful of butter. I remember the pictures hurting me and my thinking again there must be something wrong with me because everybody else is laughing and besides the library downtown has given this little book a special prize, the library lady tells us.

SO WHAT'S WRONG WITH YOU, ANY-WAY? DON'T BE SO SENSITIVE!

Sixth grade in a new catholic school and I am the first Black student. The white girls laugh at my braided hair. The nun sends a note home to my mother saying that 'pigtails are not appropriate attire for school,' and that I should learn to comb my hair in 'a more becoming style.'

Lexie Goldman and I on Lexington Avenue, our adolescent faces flushed from springtime and our dash out of high school. We stop at a luncheonette, ask for water. The woman behind the counter smiles at Lexie. Gives us water. Lexie's in a glass. Mine in a paper cup. Afterward we joke about mine being portable. Too loudly.

My first interview for a part-time job after school. An optical company on Nassau Street has called my school and asked for one of its students. The man behind the counter reads my application and then looks up at me, surprised by my Black face. His eyes remind me of the woman on the train when I was five. Then something else is added, as he looks me up and down, pausing at my breasts.

My light-skinned mother kept me alive within an environment where my life was not a high priority. She used whatever methods she had at hand, few as they were. She never talked about color. My mother was a very brave woman, born in the West Indies, unprepared for america. And she disarmed me with her silences. Somewhere I knew it was a lie that nobody else noticed color. Me, darker than my two sisters. My father, darkest of all. I was always jealous of my sisters because my mother thought they were such good girls, whereas I was bad, always in trouble. 'Full of the devil,' she used to say. They were neat, I was untidy. They were quiet, I was noisy. They were well-behaved, I was rowdy. They took piano lessons and won prizes in deportment. I stole money from my father's pockets and broke my ankle sledding downhill. They were good-looking, I was dark. Bad, mischievous, a born troublemaker if ever there was one.

Did *bad* mean *Black*? The endless scrubbing with lemon juice in the cracks and crevices of my ripening, darkening, body. And oh, the sins of my dark elbows and knees, my gums and nipples, the folds of my neck and the cave of my armpits!

The hands that grab at me from behind the stair-well are Black hands. Boys' hands, punching, rubbing, pinching, pulling at my dress. I hurl the garbage bag I'm carrying into the ashcan and jerk away, fleeing back upstairs. Hoots follow me. 'That's right, you better run, you ugly yaller bitch, just wait!' Obviously, color was relative.

My mother taught me to survive from a very early age by her own example. Her silences also taught me isolation, fury, mistrust, self-rejection, and sadness. My survival lay in learning how to use the weapons she gave me, also, to fight against those things within myself, unnamed.

And survival is the greatest gift of love. Some-times, for Black mothers, it is the only gift possible, and tenderness gets lost. My mother bore me into life as if etching an angry message into marble. Yet I survived the hatred around me because my mother made me know, by oblique reference, that no matter what went on at home, outside shouldn't oughta be the way it was. But since it was that way outside, I moved in a fen of unexplained anger that encircled me and spilled out against whomever was closest that shared those hated selves. Of course I did not realize it at the time. That anger lay like a pool of acid deep inside me, and whenever I felt deeply, I felt it, attaching itself in the strangest places. Upon those as powerless as I. My first friend asking, 'Why do you go around hitting all the time? Is that the only way you know how to be friends?'

What other creature in the world besides the Black woman has had to build the knowledge of so much hatred into her survival and keep going?

It is shortly after the Civil War. In a grey stone hospital on 110th Street in New York City a woman is screaming. She is Black, and healthy, and has been brought here from the South. I do not know her name. Her baby is ready to be born. But her legs have been tied together out of a curiosity masquerading as science. Her baby births itself to death against her bone.

Where are you seven-year-old Elizabeth Eckford of Little Rock, Arkansas? It is a bright Monday morning and you are on your way to your first day of school, draped in spittle, white hatred running down your pink sweater and a white mother's twisted mouth working – savage, inhuman – wide over your jaunty braids held high by their pink ribbons.

Numvulo has walked five days from the bleak place where the lorry deposited her. She stands in the Capetown, South Africa rain, her bare feet in the bulldozer tracks where her house once was. She picks up a piece of soaked cardboard that once covered her table and holds it over the head of her baby strapped to her back. Soon she will be arrested and taken back to the reserve, where she does not even speak the language. She will never get permission to live near her husband.

The bicentennial, in Washington, D.C. Two ample Black women stand guard over household belongings piled haphazardly onto a sidewalk in front of a house. Furniture, toys, bundles of clothes. One woman absently rocks a toy horse with the toe of her shoe, back and forth. Across the street on the side of a building opposite is a sign painted in story-high black letters, GOD HATES YOU.

Addie Mae Collins, Carol Robertson, Cynthia Wesley, Denise McNair. Four little Black girls, none more than ten years of age, singing their last autumn song in a Sunday church school in Birmingham, Alabama. After the explosion clears it is not possible to tell which patent leather Sunday shoe belongs to which found leg.

What other human being absorbs so much virulent hostility and still functions?

Black women have a history of the use and sharing of power, from the Amazon legions of Dahomey through the Ashanti warrior queen Yaa Asantewaa and the freedom fighter Harriet Tubman, to the economically powerful market-women guilds of present West Africa. We have a tradition of closeness and mutual care and support, from the all-woman courts of the Queen Mothers of Benin to the present-day Sisterhood of the Good Death, a community of old women in Brazil who, as escaped slaves, provided escape and refuge for other enslaved women, and who now care for each other.[3]

We are Black women born into a society of entrenched loathing and contempt for whatever is Black and female. We are strong and enduring. We are also deeply scarred. As African women together, we once made the earth fertile with our fingers. We can make the earth bear as well as mount the first line of fire in defense of the King. And having killed, in his name and in our own (Harriet's rifle speaks, shouldered in the grim marsh), we still know that the power to kill is less than the power to create, for it produces an ending rather than the beginning of something new.

Anger – a passion of displeasure that may be excessive or misplaced but not necessarily harmful. Hatred – an emotional habit or attitude of mind in

3. Unpublished paper by Samella Lewis.

which aversion is coupled with ill will. Anger, used, does not destroy. Hatred does.

Racism and sexism are grown-up words. Black children in america cannot avoid these distortions in their living and, too often, do not have the words for naming them. But both are correctly perceived as hatred.

Growing up, metabolizing hatred like a daily bread. Because I am Black, because I am woman, because I am not Black enough, because I am not some particular fantasy of a woman, because I AM. On such a consistent diet, one can eventually come to value the hatred of one's enemies more than one values the love of friends, for that hatred becomes the source of anger, and anger is a powerful fuel.

And true, sometimes it seems that anger alone keeps me alive; it burns with a bright and undiminished flame. Yet anger, like guilt, is an incomplete form of human knowledge. More useful than hatred, but still limited. Anger is useful to help clarify our differences, but in the long run, strength that is bred by anger alone is a blind force which cannot create the future. It can only demolish the past. Such strength does not focus upon what lies ahead, but upon what lies behind, upon what created it – hatred. And hatred is a deathwish for the hated, not a lifewish for anything else.

To grow up metabolizing hatred like daily bread means that eventually every human interaction becomes tainted with the negative passion and intensity of its byproducts – anger and cruelty.

We are African women and we know, in our blood's telling, the tenderness with which our fore-mothers held each other. It is that connection which we are seeking. We have the stories of Black women who healed each other's wounds, raised each other's children, fought each other's battles, tilled each other's earth, and eased each other's passages into life and into death. We know the possibilities of support and connection for which we all yearn, and about which we dream so often. We have a growing Black women's literature which is richly evocative of these possibilities and connections. But connections between Black women are not automatic by virtue of our similarities, and the possibilities of genuine communication between us are not easily achieved.

Often we give lip service to the idea of mutual support and connection between Black women because we have not yet crossed the barriers to these possibilities, nor fully explored the angers and fears that keep us from realizing the power of a real Black sisterhood. And to acknowledge our dreams is to sometimes acknowledge the distance between those dreams and our present situation. Acknowledged, our dreams can shape the realities of our future, if we arm them with the hard work and scrutiny of now. We cannot settle for the pretenses of connection, or for parodies of self-love. We cannot continue to evade each other on the deepest levels because we fear each other's angers, nor continue to believe that respect means never looking directly nor with openness into another Black woman's eyes.

I was not meant to be alone and without you who understand.[4]

I

I know the anger that lies inside of me like I know the beat of my heart and the taste of my spit. It is easier to be angry than to hurt. Anger is what I do best. It is easier to be furious than to be yearning. Easier to crucify myself in you than to take on the threatening universe of whiteness by admitting that we are worth wanting each other.

As Black women, we have shared so many similar experiences. Why doesn't this commonality bring us closer together instead of setting us at each

4. From 'Letters from Black Feminists, 1972–1978' by Barbara Smith and Beverly Smith in *Conditions: Four* (1979).

other's throats with weapons well-honed by familiarity?

The anger with which I meet another Black woman's slightest deviation from my immediate need or desire or concept of a proper response is a deep and hurtful anger, chosen only in the sense of a choice of desperation – reckless through despair. That anger which masks my pain that we are so separate who should most be together – my pain – that she could perhaps not need me as much as I need her, or see me through the blunted eye of the haters, that eye I know so well from my own distorted images of her. Erase or be erased!

I stand in the Public Library waiting to be recognized by the Black woman library clerk seated a few feet behind the desk. She seems engrossed in a book, beautiful in her youth and self-assuredness. I straighten my glasses, giving a tiny shake to my bangles in the process just in case she has not seen me, but I somehow know she has. Otherwise motionless, she slowly turns her head and looks up. Her eyes cross mine with a look of such incidental hostility that I feel pilloried to the wall. Two male patrons enter behind me. At that, she rises and moves toward me. 'Yes,' she says, with no inflection at all, her eyes carefully elsewhere. I've never seen this young woman before in my life. I think to myself, 'now that's what you call an attitude,' recognizing the rising tension inside of me.

The art, beyond insolence, of the Black girl's face as she cuts her elegant sidelong glance at me. What makes her eyes slide off of mine? What does she see that angers her so, or infuriates her, or disgusts her? Why do I want to break her face off when her eyes do not meet mine? Why does she wear my sister's face? My daughter's mouth turned down about to suck itself in? The eyes of a furious and rejected lover? Why do I dream I cradle you at night? Divide your limbs between the food bowls of my least favorite animals? Keep vigil for you night after terrible night, wondering? Oh sister, where is that dark rich land we wanted to wander through together?

Hate said the voice wired in 3/4 time printed in dirty type all the views fit to kill, me and you, me or you. And whose future image have we destroyed – your face or mine – without either how shall I look again at both – lacking either is lacking myself.

And if I trust you what pale dragon will you feed our brown flesh to from fear, self-preservation, or to what brothered altar all innocent of loving that has no place to go and so becomes another face of terror or of hate?

A dumb beast endlessly recording inside the poisonous attacks of silence – meat gone wrong – what could ever grow in that dim lair and how does the child convert from sacrifice to liar?

My blood sister, across her living room from me. Sitting back in her chair while I talk earnestly, trying to reach her, trying to alter the perceptions of me that cause her so much pain. Slowly, carefully, and coldly, so I will not miss one single scathing word, she says, 'I am not interested in understanding whatever you're trying to say – I don't care to hear it.'

I have never gotten over the anger that you did not want me as a sister, nor an ally, nor even a diversion one cut above the cat. You have never gotten over the anger that I appeared at all. And that I am different, but not different enough. One woman has eyes like my sister who never forgave me for appearing before she had a chance to win her mother's love, as if anybody ever could. Another woman wears the high cheekbones of my other sister who wanted to lead but had only been taught to obey, so now she is dedicated to ruling by obedience, a passive vision.

Who did we expect the other to be who is not yet at peace with our own selves? I cannot shut you out the way I shut the others out so maybe I can destroy you. Must destroy you?

We do not love ourselves, therefore we cannot

love each other. Because we see in each other's face our own face, the face we never stopped wanting. Because we survived and survival breeds desire for more self. A face we never stopped wanting at the same time as we try to obliterate it.

Why don't we meet each other's eyes? Do we expect betrayal in each other's gaze, or recognition?

If just once we were to feel the pain of all Black women's blood flooding up to drown us! I stayed afloat buoyed by an anger so deep at my loneliness that I could only move toward further survival.

When one cannot influence a situation it is an act of wisdom to withdraw.[5]

Every Black woman in america has survived several lifetimes of hatred, where even in the candy store cases of our childhood, little brown nigger-baby candies testified against us. We survived the wind-driven spittle on our child's shoe and pink flesh-colored bandaids, attempted rapes on rooftops and the prodding fingers of the super's boy, seeing our girlfriends blown to bits in Sunday School, and we absorbed that loathing as a natural state. We had to metabolize such hatred that our cells have learned to live upon it because we had to, or die of

5. From *The I Ching*.

it. Old King Mithridates learned to eat arsenic bit by bit and so outwitted his poisoners, but I'd have hated to kiss him upon his lips! Now we deny such hatred ever existed because we have learned to neutralize it through ourselves, and the catabolic process throws off waste products of fury even when we love.

> I see hatred
> I am bathed in it, drowning in it
> since almost the beginning of my life
> it has been the air I breathe
> the food I eat, the content of my perceptions;
> the single most constant fact of my existence
> is their hatred . . .
> I am too young for my history[6]

It is not that Black women shed each other's psychic blood so easily, but that we have ourselves bled so often, the pain of bloodshed becomes almost commonplace. If I have learned to eat my own flesh in the forest – starving, keening, learning the lesson of the she-wolf who chews off her own paw to leave the trap behind – if I must drink my own blood, thirsting, why should I stop at yours until your dear dead

6. From 'Nigger' by Judy Dothard Simmons in *Decent Intentions* (Blind Beggar Press, New York, 1983).

arms hang like withered garlands upon my breast and I weep for your going, oh my sister, I grieve for our gone.

When an error of oversight allows one of us to escape without the full protective dose of fury and air of contemptuous disdain, when she approaches us without a measure of distrust and reserve flowing from her pores, or without her eyes coloring each appraisal of us with that unrelenting sharpness and suspicion reserved only for each other, when she approaches without sufficient caution, then she is cursed by the first accusation of derision – *naive* – meaning not programmed for defensive attack before inquiry. Even more than *confused, naive* is the ultimate wipeout between us.

Black women eating our own hearts out for nourishment in an empty house empty compound empty city in an empty season, and for each of us one year the spring will not return – we learned to savor the taste of our own flesh before any other because that was all that was allowed us. And we have become to each other unmentionably dear and immeasurably dangerous. I am writing about an anger so huge and implacable, so corrosive, it must destroy what it most needs for its own solution, dis-solution, resolution. Here we are attempting to address each others' eyes directly. Even if our words taste sharp as the edge of a lost woman's voice, we are speaking.

II

A Black woman, working her years, committed to life as she lives it, the children fed and clothed and loved as she can into some strength that does not allow them to encyst like horse chestnuts, knowing all the time from the start that she must either kill them or eventually send them into the deathlands, the white labyrinth.

I sat at our Thanksgiving Day table listening to my daughter talk about the university and the horrors of determined invisibility. Over the years I have recorded her dreams of death at their hands, sometimes glorious, sometimes cheap. She tells me of the teachers who refuse to understand simple questions, who look at her as if she were a benign – meaning powerless – but unsightly tumor. She weeps. I hold her. I tell her to remember the university doesn't own her, that she has a home. But I have let her go into that jungle of ghosts, having taught her only how to be fleet of foot, how to whistle, how to love, and how not to run. Unless she has to. It is never enough.

Black women give our children forth into a hatred that seared our own young days with bewilderment, hoping we have taught them something they can use to fashion their own new and less costly pathways to survival. Knowing I did not slit their throats at birth, tear out the tiny beating heart with my own despairing teeth the way some sisters did in the slaveships chained to corpses and therefore was I committed to this very moment.

The price of increasing power is increasing opposition.[7]

I sat listening to my girl talk about the bent world she was determined to reenter in spite of all she was saying, because she views a knowledge of that world as part of an arsenal which she can use to change it all. I listened, hiding my pained need to snatch her back into the web of my smaller protections. I sat watching while she worked it out bit by hurtful bit – what she really wanted – feeling her rage wax and wane, feeling her anger building against me because I could not help her do it nor do it for her, nor would she allow that.

All mothers see their daughters leaving. Black mothers see it happening as a sacrifice through the veil of hatred hung like sheets of lava in the pathway before their daughters. All daughters see their

7. From *The I Ching*.

mothers leaving. Black girls see it happening through a veil of threatened isolation no fire of trusting pierces.

Last month I held another Black woman in my arms as she sobbed out the grief and deprivation of her mother's death. Her inconsolable loss – the emptiness of the emotional landscape she was seeing in front of her – spoke out of her mouth from a place of untouchable aloneness that could never admit another Black woman close enough again to matter. 'The world is divided into two kinds of people,' she said, 'those who have mothers and those who don't. And I don't have a mother anymore.' What I heard her saying was that no other Black woman would ever see who she was, ever trust or be trusted by her again. I heard in her cry of loneliness the source of the romance between Black women and our mommas.

Little Black girls, tutored by hate into wanting to become anything else. We cut our eyes at sister because she can only reflect what everybody else except momma seemed to know – that we were hateful, or ugly, or worthless, but certainly unblessed. We were not boys and we were not white, so we counted for less than nothing, except to our mommas.

If we can learn to give ourselves the recognition

and acceptance that we have come to expect only from our mommas, Black women will be able to see each other much more clearly and deal with each other much more directly.

I think about the harshness that exists so often within the least encounter between Black women, the judgment and the sizing up, that cruel refusal to connect. I know sometimes I feel like it is worth my life to disagree with another Black woman. Better to ignore her, withdraw from her, go around her, just don't deal with her. Not just because she irritates me, but because she might destroy me with the cruel force of her response to what must feel like an affront, namely me. Or I might destroy her with the force of mine, for the very same reason. The fears are equal.

Once I can absorb the particulars of my life as a Black woman, and multiply them by my two children and all the days of our collective Black lives, and I do not falter beneath the weight – what Black woman is not a celebration, like water, like sunlight, like rock – is it any wonder that my voice is harsh? Now to require of myself the effort of awareness, so that harshness will not function in the places it is least deserved – toward my sisters.

Why do Black women reserve a particular voice of fury and disappointment for each other? Who is it we must destroy when we attack each other with that tone of predetermined and correct annihilation? We reduce one another to our own lowest common denominator, and then we proceed to try and obliterate what we most desire to love and touch, the problematic self, unclaimed but fiercely guarded from the other.

This cruelty between us, this harshness, is a piece of the legacy of hate with which we were inoculated from the time we were born by those who intended it to be an injection of death. But we adapted, learned to take it in and use it, unscrutinized. Yet at what cost! In order to withstand the weather, we had to become stone, and now we bruise ourselves upon the other who is closest.

How do I alter course so each Black woman's face I meet is not the face of my mother or my killer?

I loved you. I dreamed about you. I talked to you for hours in my sleep sitting under a silk-cotton tree our arms around each other or braiding each other's hair or oiling each other's backs, and every time I run into you on the street or at the post office or behind the Medicaid desk I want to wring your neck.

There are so many occasions in each of our lives for righteous fury, multiplied and dividing.

- Black women being told that we can be somehow better, and are worse, but never equal. To Black men. To other women. To human beings.

- The white academic feminist who tells me she is so glad *This Bridge Called My Back*[8] exists, because now it gives her a chance to deal with racism without having to face the harshness of Black undiluted by other colors. What she means is she does not have to examine her own specific terror and loathing of Blackness, nor deal with the angers of Black women. So get away with your dirty ugly mean faces, all screwed up all the time!

- The racist filmstrip artist who I thought I had handled so patiently and well. I didn't blow up his damned machine. I explained how his racial blindness made me feel and how his film could be altered to have some meaning. He probably learned something about showing Black images. Then I came home and almost tore up my house and my lover because some invitations happened to be misprinted. Not seeing where the charge of rage was born.

- A convicted Black man, a torturer of women and

8. *This Bridge Called My Back: Writings by Radical Women of Color* edited by Cherrie Moraga and Gloria Anzaldua (Kitchen Table: Women of Color Press, New York, 1984).

children, army-trained to be a killer, writes in his journal in his death cell: 'I am the type of person you are most likely to find driving a Mercedes and sitting in the executive offices of 100 big corporations.' And he's right. Except he's Black.

How do we keep from releasing our angers at them upon ourselves and each other? How do I free myself from this poison I was force-fed like a Strasburg goose until I vomited anger at the least scent of anything nourishing, *oh my sister the belligerent lift of your shoulder the breath of your hair* . . . We each learned the craft of destruction. It is all they knew to allow us, yet look how our words are finding each other again.

It is difficult to construct a wholesomeness model when we are surrounded with synonyms for filth. But not impossible. We have, after all, survived for a reason. (How do I define my impact upon this earth?) I begin by searching for the right questions.

Dear Leora,

For two Black women to enter an analytic or therapeutic relationship means beginning an essentially uncharted and insecure journey. There are no prototypes, no models, no objectively accessible body of experience other than ourselves by which to examine the specific dynamics of our interactions as Black women. Yet this interaction can affect all the other psychic matter attended profoundly. It is to scrutinize that very interaction that I sought you out professionally, and I have come to see that it means picking my way through our similarities and our differences, as well as through our histories of calculated mistrust and desire.

Because it has not been done before or at least not been noted, this particular scrutiny is painful and fraught with the vulnerability of all psychic scrutinies plus all of the pitfalls created by our being Black women in a white male world, and Black women who have survived. This is a scrutiny often sidestepped or considered unimportant or beside the point. EXAMPLE: I can't tell you how many good white psychwomen have said to me, 'Why should it matter if I am Black or white?' who would never think of saying, 'Why does it matter if I am female or male?' EXAMPLE: I don't know who you are in supervision with, but I can bet it's not with another Black woman.

So this territory between us feels new and frightening as well as urgent, rigged with detonating pieces of our own individual racial histories which neither of us chose but which each of us bears the scars from. And those are particular to each of us. But there is a history which we share because we are Black women in a racist sexist cauldron, and that means some part of this journey is yours, also.

I have many troubled areas of self that will be neither new nor problematic to you as a trained and capable psychperson. I think you are a brave woman and I respect that, yet I doubt that your training can have prepared you to explore the tangle of need, fear, distrust, despair, and hope which operates between us, and certainly not to the depth necessary. Because neither of us is male nor white, we belong to a group of human beings that has not been thought worthy of that kind of study. So we have only who we are, with or without the courage to use those selves for further exploration and clarification of how what lies between us as Black women affects us and the work we do together.

Yet if we do not do it here between us, each one of us will have to do it somewhere else, sometime.

I know these things: I do not yet know what to do about them. But I do want to make them fit together to serve my life and my work, and I don't mean merely in a way that feels safe. I don't know how they can further and illuminate your life and work, but I know they can. It is sometimes both the curse and the blessing of the poet to perceive without yet being able to order those perceptions, and that is another name for Chaos.

But of course it is out of Chaos that new worlds are born.

I look forward to our meeting eye to eye.

Audre

III

There has been so much death and loss around me recently, without metaphor or redeeming symbol, that sometimes I feel trapped into one idiom only – that one of suffering and its codicil, to bear. The same problem exists with anger. I have processed too much of it recently, or else the machinery is slowing down or becoming less efficient, and it creeps into my most crucial interchanges.

Perhaps this is why it is often easier for Black women to interact with white women, even though those interactions are often a dead end emotionally. For with white women there is a middle depth of interaction possible and sustainable, an emotional limit to relationships of self upon self acknowledged.

Now why is this not so with Frances, who is white, and whom I meet at a depth beyond anyone? When I speak of Frances and me I am talking about a relationship not only of great depth but one of great breadth also, a totaling of differences without merging. I am also speaking of a love shaped by our mutual commitment to hard work and confrontation over many years, each of us refusing to settle for what was easy, or simple, or acceptably convenient.

That middle depth of relationship more usually possible between Black and white women, however, is less threatening than the tangle of unexplored needs and furies that face any two Black women who seek to engage each other directly, emotionally, no matter what the context of their relationship may be. This holds true for office workers and political activists as well as lovers. But it is through threading this tangle that new visions of self and possibility between Black women emerge. Again, I am speaking here of social relationships, for it is crucial that we examine dynamics between women who are not lovers as well as between women who are.

I ask myself, do I ever use my war against racism

to avoid other even more unanswerable pain? And if so, doesn't that make the energy behind my battles against racism sometimes more tenuous, or less clearheaded, or subject to unexpected stresses and disappointments? White people can never truly validate us. For example: At this point in time, were racism to be totally eradicated from those middle range relationships between Black women and white women, those relationships might become deeper, but they would still never satisfy our particular Black woman's need for one another, given our shared knowledge and traditions and history. There are two very different struggles involved here. One is the war against racism in white people, and the other is the need for Black women to confront and wade through the racist constructs underlying our deprivation of each other. And these battles are not at all the same.

But sometimes it feels like better a righteous fury than the dull ache of loss, loss, loss. My daughter leaving her time of daughter-hood. Friends going away in one way or another.

. . . as those seemingly alike in nature, nature emphasizes their uniqueness and the differences become more obvious.[9]

9. From *The I Ching*.

How often have I demanded from another Black woman what I had not dared to give myself – acceptance, faith, enough space to consider change? How often have I asked her to leap across difference, suspicion, distrust, old pain? How many times have I expected her to jump the hideous gaps of our learned despisals alone, like an animal trained through blindness to ignore the precipice? How many times have I forgotten to ask this question?

Am I not reaching out for you in the only language I know? Are you reaching for me in your only salvaged tongue? If I try to hear yours across our differences does/will that mean you can hear mine?

Do we explore these questions or do we settle for that secret isolation which is the learned tolerance of deprivation of each other – that longing for each other's laughter, dark ease, sharing, and permission to be ourselves that we do not admit to feeling, usually, because then we would have to admit the lack; and the pain of that lacking, persistent as a low-grade fever and as debilitating?

Do we reenact these crucifixions upon each other, the avoidance, the cruelty, the judgments, because we have not been allowed Black goddesses, Black heroines; because we have not been allowed to see our mothers and our selves in their/our own magnificence until that magnificence became part of our blood and bone? One of the functions of hatred is certainly to mask and distort the beauty which is power in ourselves.

I am hungry for Black women who will not turn from me in anger and contempt even before they know me or hear what I have to say. I am hungry for Black women who will not turn away from me even if they do not agree with what I say. We are, after all, talking about different combinations of the same borrowed sounds.

Sometimes exploring our differences feels like marching out to war. I hurl myself with trepidation into the orbit of every Black woman I want to reach, advancing with the best of what I have to offer held out at arm's length before me – myself. Does it feel different to her? At the same time as I am terrified, expecting betrayal, rejection, the condemnations of laughter, is she feeling judged by me?

Most of the Black women I know think I cry too much, or that I'm too public about it. I've been told that crying makes me seem soft and therefore of little consequence. As if our softness has to be the price we pay out for power, rather than simply the one that's paid most easily and most often.

I fight nightmare images inside my own self, see

them, own them, know they did not destroy me before and will not destroy me now if I speak them out, admit how they have scarred me, that my mother taught me to survive at the same time as she taught me to fear my own Blackness. 'Don't trust white people because they mean us no good and don't trust anyone darker than you because their hearts are as Black as their faces.' (And where did that leave me, the darkest one?) It is painful even now to write it down. How many messages like that come down to all of us, and in how many different voices, how many different ways? And how can we expunge these messages from our consciousness without first recognizing what it was they were saying, and how destructive they were?

IV

What does it take to be tough? Learned cruelty?

Now there is bound to be a voice saying that Black women have always helped one another, haven't we? And that is the paradox of our inner conflict. We have a strong and ancient tradition of bonding and mutual support, and the memorized threads of that tradition exist within each of us, in opposition to the anger and suspicion engendered by self-hate.

When the world moved against me with a disapproving frown/It was sister put the ground back under my feet.[10]

Hearing those words sung has always provoked the most profound and poignant sense of loss within me for something I wanted to feel and could not because it had never happened for me. There are some Black women for whom it has. For others of us, that sense of being able to depend upon rock bottom support from our sisters is something we dream about and work toward, knowing it is possible, but also very problematic across the realities of fear and suspicion lying between us.

Our anger, tempered over survival fires, shuttered behind downcast eyelids, or else blazing out of our eyes at the oddest times. Looking up from between the legs of a lover, over a notebook in the middle of a lecture and I almost lost my train of thought, ringing up groceries in the supermarket, filling out the form behind the unemployment office window, stepping out of a cab in the middle of Broadway on the arm of a businessman from Lagos, sweeping ahead of me into a shop as I open the door,

10. From 'Every Woman Ever Loved A Woman' by Bernice Johnson Reagon, song performed by Sweet Honey in the Rock.

looking into each others eyes for a split second only – furious, cutting, sisters. My daughter asking me all the time when she was a little girl, 'Are you angry about something, Mommy?'

As Black women, we have wasted our angers too often, buried them, called them someone else's, cast them wildly into oceans of racism and sexism from which no vibration resounded, hurled them into each other's teeth and then ducked to avoid the impact. But by and large, we avoid open expression of them, or cordon them off in a rigid and un-approachable politeness. The rage that feels illicit or unjustified is kept secret, unnamed, and preserved forever. We are stuffed with furies, against our-selves, against each other, terrified to examine them lest we find ourselves in bold print fingered and named what we have always felt and even some-times preferred ourselves to be – alone. And certainly, there are enough occasions in all our lives where we can use our anger righteously, enough for many lifetimes. We can avoid confrontation with each other very readily. It is so much easier to examine our anger within situations that are (rela-tively) clearcut and emotionally unloaded. It is so much easier to express our anger in those middle depth relationships that do not threaten genuine self-exposure. And yet always that hunger for the substance known, a hunger for the real shared, for the sister who shares.

It is hard to stand up in the teeth of white dismissal and aggression, of gender hatred and attack. It is so much harder to tackle face-on the rejection of Black women who may be seeing in my face some face they have not discarded in their own mirror, who see in my eyes the shape they have come to fear may be their own. So often this fear is stoked between Black women by the feared loss of a male companion, present or sought after. For we have also been taught that a man acquired was the sole measure of success, and yet they almost never stay.

One Black woman sits and silently judges another, how she looks, how she acts, how she impresses others. The first woman's scales are weighted against herself. She is measuring the impossible. She is measuring the self she does not fully want to be. She does not want to accept the contradictions, nor the beauty. She wishes the other woman would go away. She wishes the other woman would become someone else, anyone other than another Black woman. She has enough trouble dealing with being herself. 'Why don't you learn to fly straight,' she says to the other woman. 'Don't you understand what your poor showing says about us all? If I could fly I'd certainly do a better job than *that*. Can't you put on a more together show? The white girls do it. Maybe we could get one to show you how.' The other woman cannot speak. She is too busy keeping herself from crashing upon the ground. She will not cry the tears which are hardening into little sharp stones that spit from her eyes and implant themselves in the first woman's heart, who quickly heals over them and identifies them as the source of her pain.

v

There are myths of self-protection that hold us separate from each other and breed harshness and cruelty where we most need softness and understanding.

1. That courtesy or politeness require our not noticing each other directly, only with the most covert of evaluating glances. At all costs, we must avoid the image of our fear. 'How beautiful your mouth is' might well be heard as 'Look at those big lips.' We maintain a discreet distance us makes me less you, makes you less me.

When there is no connection at all between people, then anger is a way of bringing them closer together, of making contact. But when there is a great deal of connectedness that is problematic or threatening or unacknowledged, then anger is a way of keeping people separate, of putting distance between us.

2. That because we sometimes rise to each other's defense against outsiders, we do not need to look at devaluation and dismissal among ourselves. Support against outsiders is very different from cherishing each other. Often it is a case of 'like needs like.' It doesn't mean we have to appreciate that *like* or our need of it, even when that *like* is the only thin line between dying and living.

For if I take the white world's estimation of me as Black-woman-synonymous-with-garbage to heart, then deep down inside myself I will always believe that I am truly good for nothing. But it is very hard to look absorbed hatred in the face. It is easier to see you as good for nothing because you are like me. So when you support me because you are like me, that merely confirms that you are nothing too, just like me. It's a no-win position, a case of nothing supporting nothing and someone's gonna have to pay for that one, and it sure ain't gonna be me! When I can recognize my worth, I can recognize yours.

3. That perfection is possible, a correct expectation from ourselves and each other, and the only terms of acceptance, humanness. (Note how very useful

that makes us to the external institutions!) If you are like me, then you will have to be a lot better than I am in order to even be good enough. And you can't be because no matter how good you are you're still a Black woman, just like me. (Who does she think she is?) So any act or idea that I could accept or at least examine from anyone else is not even tolerable if it comes from you, my mirror image. If you are not THEIR image of perfection, and you can't ever be because you are a Black woman, then you are a reflection upon me. We are never good enough for each other. All your faults become magnified reflections of my own threatening inadequacies. I must attack you first before our enemies confuse us with each other. But they will anyway.

Oh mother, why were we armed to fight with cloud-wreathed swords and javelins of dust? 'Just who do you think you are, anyway?' Who I am most afraid of (never) meeting.

VI

The language by which we have been taught to dismiss ourselves and our feelings as suspect is the same language we use to dismiss and suspect each other. Too pretty – too ugly. Too Black – too white. Wrong. I already know that. Who says so. You're too questionable for me to hear you. You speak THEIR language. You don't speak THEIR language. Who do you think you are? You think you're better than anybody else? Get out of my face.

We refuse to give up the artificial distances between us, or to examine our real differences for creative exchange. I'm too different for us to communicate. Meaning, I must establish myself as not-you. And the road to anger is paved with our unexpressed fear of each other's judgment. We have not been allowed to experience each other freely as Black women in america; we come to each other coated in myths, stereotypes, and expectations from the outside, definitions not our own. 'You are my reference group, but I have never worked with you.' How are you judging me? As Black as you? Blacker than you? Not Black enough? Whichever, I am going to be found wanting in some way . . .

We are Black women, defined as never-good-enough. I must overcome that by becoming better than you. If I expect enough from myself, then maybe I can become different enough, then maybe I won't be a 'nigger bitch' anymore. If I make you different enough from me, then I won't need you so much. I will become strong, the best, excel in everything, become the very best because I don't dare to be anything else. It is my only chance to become good enough to become human.

If I am myself, then you cannot accept me. But if you can accept me, that means I am what you would like to be, and then I'm not 'the real thing.' But then neither are you. WILL THE REAL BLACK WOMAN PLEASE STAND UP?

We cherish our guilty secret, buried under exquisite clothing and expensive makeup and bleaching creams (yes, still!) and hair straighteners masquerading as permanent waves. The killer instinct toward any one of us who deviates from the prescribed cover is precise and deadly.

Acting like an insider and feeling like the outsider, preserving our self-rejection as Black women at the same time as we're getting over – we think. And political work will not save our souls, no matter how correct and necessary that work is. Yet it is true that without political work we cannot hope to survive long enough to effect any change. And self-empowerment is the most deeply political work there is, and the most difficult.

When we do not attempt to name the confusion of feelings which exist between sisters, we act them out in hundreds of hurtful and unproductive ways. Never speaking from the old pain, to beyond. As if we have made a secret pact between ourselves not to speak, for the expression of that unexamined pain might be accompanied by other ancient and unexpressed hurtings embedded in the stored-up anger we have not expressed. And that anger, as we know from our flayed egos of childhood, is armed with a powerful cruelty learned in the bleakness of too-early battles for survival. 'You can't take it, huh!' The Dozens. A Black game of supposedly friendly rivalry and name-calling; in reality, a crucial exercise in learning how to absorb verbal abuse without faltering.

A piece of the price we paid for learning survival was our childhood. We were never allowed to be children. It is the right of children to be able to play at living for a little while, but for a Black child, every act can have deadly serious consequences, and for a Black girl child, even more so. Ask the ghosts of the four little Black girls blown up in Birmingham. Ask Angel Lenair, or Latonya Wilson, or Cynthia Montgomery, the three girl victims in the infamous Atlanta murders, none of whose deaths have ever been solved.

Sometimes it feels as if I were to experience all the collective hatred that I have had directed at me as a Black woman, admit its implications into my consciousness, I might die of the bleak and horrible weight. Is that why a sister once said to me, 'white people feel, Black people do'?

It is true that in america white people, by and large, have more time and space to afford the luxury of scrutinizing their emotions. Black people in this country have always had to attend closely to the hard and continuous work of survival in the most material and immediate planes. But it is a temptation to move from this fact to the belief that Black people do not need to examine our feelings; or that they are unimportant, since they have so often been used to stereotype and infantalize us; or that these feelings are not vital to our survival; or, worse, that there is some acquired virtue in not feeling them deeply. That is carrying a timebomb wired to our emotions.

There is a distinction I am beginning to make in my living between *pain* and *suffering*. Pain is an event, an experience that must be recognized, named, and then used in some way in order for the experience to change, to be transformed into something else, strength or knowledge or action.

Suffering, on the other hand, is the nightmare reliving of unscrutinized and unmetabolized pain. When I live through pain without recognizing it, self-consciously, I rob myself of the power that can come from using that pain, the power to fuel some movement beyond it. I condemn myself to reliving that pain over and over and over whenever something close triggers it. And that is suffering, a seemingly inescapable cycle.

And true, experiencing old pain sometimes feels like hurling myself full force against a concrete wall. But I remind myself that I HAVE LIVED THROUGH IT ALL ALREADY, AND SURVIVED.

Sometimes the anger that lies between Black women is not examined because we spend so much of our substance having to examine others constantly in the name of self-protection and survival, and we cannot reserve enough energy to scrutinize ourselves. Sometimes we don't do it because the anger's been there so long we don't know what it is, or we think it's natural to suffer rather than to experience pain. Sometimes, because we are afraid of what we will find. Sometimes, because we don't think we deserve it.

The revulsion on the woman's face in the subway as she moves her coat away and I think she is seeing a roach. But I see the hatred in her eyes because she wants me to see the hatred in her eyes, because she wants me to know in the way only a child can know that I don't belong alive in her world. If I'd been grown, I'd probably have laughed or snarled or been hurt, seen it for what it was. But I am five years old.

I see it, I record it, I do not name it, so the experience is incomplete. It is not pain; it becomes suffering.

And how can I tell you I don't like the way you cut your eyes at me if I know that I am going to release all the unnamed angers within you spawned by the hatred you have suffered and never felt?

So we are drawn to each other but wary, demanding the instant perfection we would never expect from our enemies. But it is possible to break through this inherited agony, to refuse acquiescence in this bitter charade of isolation and anger and pain.

I read this question many times in the letters of Black women, 'Why do I feel myself to be such an anathema, so isolated?' I hear it spoken over and over again, in endless covert ways. But we can change that scenario. We can learn to mother ourselves.

What does that mean for Black women? It means we must establish authority over our own definition, provide an attentive concern and expectation of growth which is the beginning of that acceptance we came to expect only from our mothers. It means that I affirm my own worth by committing myself to my own survival, in my own self and in the self of other Black women. On the other hand, it means that as I learn my worth and genuine possibility, I refuse to settle for anything less than a rigorous pursuit of the possible in myself, at the same time making a distinction between what is possible and what the outside world drives me to do in order to prove I am human. It means being able to recognize my successes, and to be tender with myself, even when I fail.

We will begin to see each other as we dare to begin to see ourselves; we will begin to see ourselves as we begin to see each other, without aggrandizement or dismissal or recriminations, but with patience and understanding for when we do not quite make it, and recognition and appreciation for when we do. Mothering ourselves means learning how to be both kind and demanding in the teeth of failure as well as in the face of success, and not mis-naming either.

When you come to respect the character of the time you will not have to cover emptiness with pretense.[11]

We must recognize and nuture the creative parts of each other without always understanding what will be created.

As we fear each other less and value each other more, we will come to value recognition within each other's eyes as well as within our own, and seek a balance between these visions. Mothering. Claiming some power over who we choose to be,

11. From *The I Ching*.

and knowing that such power is relative within the realities of our lives. Yet knowing that only through the use of that power can we effectively change those realities. Mothering means the laying to rest of what is weak, timid, and damaged – without despisal – the protection and support of what is useful for survival and change, and our joint explorations of the difference.

I recall a beautiful and intricate sculpture from the court of the Queen Mother of Benin, entitled 'The Power Of The Hand.' It depicts the Queen Mother, her court women, and her warriors in a circular celebration of the human power to achieve success in practical and material ventures, the ability to make something out of anything. In Dahomey, that power is female.

VII

Theorizing about self-worth is ineffective. So is pretending. Women can die in agony who have lived with blank and beautiful faces. I can afford to look at myself directly, risk the pain of experiencing who I am not, and learn to savor the sweetness of who I am. I can make friends with all the different pieces of me, liked and disliked. Admit that I am kinder to my neighbor's silly husband most days than I am to myself. I can look into the mirror and learn to love the stormy little Black girl who once longed to be white or anything other than who she was, since all she was ever allowed to be was the sum of the color of her skin and the textures of her hair, the shade of her knees and elbows, and those things were clearly not acceptable as human.

Learning to love ourselves as Black women goes beyond a simplistic insistence that 'Black is beautiful.' It goes beyond and deeper than a surface appreciation of Black beauty, although that is certainly a good beginning. But if the quest to reclaim ourselves and each other remains there, then we risk another superficial measurement of self, one superimposed upon the old one and almost as damaging, since it pauses at the superficial. Certainly it is no more empowering. And it is empowerment – our strengthening in the service of ourselves and each other, in the service of our work and future – that will be the result of this pursuit.

I have to learn to love myself before I can love you or accept your loving. You have to learn to love yourself before you can love me or accept my loving. Know we are worthy of touch before we can reach out for each other. Not cover that sense of worthlessness with 'I don't want you' or 'it doesn't matter' or 'white folks feel, Black folks DO.' And these are enormously difficult to accomplish in an environment that consistently encourages nonlove and coverup, an environment that warns us to be quiet about our need of each other, by defining our dissatisfactions as unanswerable and our necessities as unobtainable.

Until now, there has been little that taught us how to be kind to each other. To the rest of the world, yes, but not to ourselves. There have been few external examples of how to treat another Black woman with kindness, deference, tenderness or an appreciative smile in passing, just because she IS; an understanding of each other's shortcomings because we have been somewhere close to that, ourselves. When last did you compliment another sister, give recognition to her specialness? We have to consciously study how to be tender with each other until it becomes a habit because what was native has been stolen from us, the love of Black women for each other. But we can practice being gentle with each other. We can practice being gentle with each other by being gentle with that piece of ourselves that is hardest to hold, by giving more to the brave bruised girlchild within each of us, by expecting a little less from her gargantuan efforts to excel. We can love her in the light as well as in the darkness, quiet her frenzy toward perfection and encourage her attentions toward fulfillment. Maybe then we will come to appreciate more how much she has taught us, and how much she is doing to keep this world revolving toward some livable future.

It would be ridiculous to believe that this process is not lengthy and difficult. It is suicidal to believe it is not possible. As we arm ourselves with ourselves and each other, we can stand toe to toe inside that rigorous loving and begin to speak the impossible – of what has always seemed like the impossible – to one another. The first step toward genuine change. Eventually, if we speak the truth to each other, it will become unavoidable to ourselves.

Age, Race, Class, and Sex: Women Redefining Difference[1]

Much of Western European history conditions us to see human differences in simplistic opposition to each other: dominant/subordinate, good/bad, up/down, superior/inferior. In a society where the good is defined in terms of profit rather than in terms of human need, there must always be some group of people who, through systematized oppression, can be made to feel surplus, to occupy the place of the dehumanized inferior. Within this society, that group is made up of Black and Third World people, working-class people, older people, and women.

As a forty-nine-year-old Black lesbian feminist socialist mother of two, including one boy, and a member of an interracial couple, I usually find myself a part of some group defined as other, deviant, inferior, or just plain wrong. Traditionally, in

1. Paper delivered at the Copeland Colloquium, Amherst College, April 1980.

american society, it is the members of oppressed, objectified groups who are expected to stretch out and bridge the gap between the actualities of our lives and the consciousness of our oppressor. For in order to survive, those of us for whom oppression is as american as apple pie have always had to be watchers, to become familiar with the language and manners of the oppressor, even sometimes adopting them for some illusion of protection. Whenever the need for some pretense of communication arises, those who profit from our oppression call upon us to share our knowledge with them. In other words, it is the responsibility of the oppressed to teach the oppressors their mistakes. I am responsible for educating teachers who dismiss my children's culture in school. Black and Third World people are expected to educate white people as to our humanity. Women are expected to educate men. Lesbians and gay men are expected to educate the heterosexual world. The oppressors maintain their position and evade responsibility for their own actions. There is a constant drain of energy which might be better used in redefining ourselves and devising realistic scenarios for altering the present and constructing the future.

Institutionalized rejection of difference is an absolute necessity in a profit economy which needs outsiders as surplus people. As members of such an economy, we have all been programmed to respond to the human differences between us with fear and loathing and to handle that difference in one of three ways: ignore it, and if that is not possible, copy it if we think it is dominant, or destroy it if we think it is subordinate. But we have no patterns for relating across our human differences as equals. As a result, those differences have been misnamed and misused in the service of separation and confusion.

Certainly there are very real differences between us of race, age, and sex. But it is not those differences between us that are separating us. It is rather our refusal to recognize those differences, and to examine the distortions which result from our misnaming them and their effects upon human behavior and expectation.

Racism, the belief in the inherent superiority of one race over all others and thereby the right to dominance. Sexism, the belief in the inherent superiority of one sex over the other and thereby the right to dominance. Ageism. Heterosexism. Elitism. Classism.

It is a lifetime pursuit for each one of us to extract these distortions from our living at the same time as we recognize, reclaim, and define those differences upon which they are imposed. For we have all been raised in a society where those distortions were endemic within our living. Too often, we pour the energy needed for recognizing and exploring difference into pretending those differences are insurmountable barriers, or that they do not exist at all. This results in a voluntary isolation, or false and treacherous connections. Either way, we do not develop tools for using human difference as a springboard for creative change within our lives. We speak not of human difference, but of human deviance.

Somewhere, on the edge of consciousness, there is what I call a *mythical norm*, which each one of us within our heart knows 'that is not me.' In america, this norm is usually defined as white, thin, male, young, heterosexual, christian, and financially secure. It is with this mythical norm that the trappings of power reside within this society. Those of us who stand outside that power often identify one way in which we are different, and we assume that to be the primary cause of all oppression, forgetting other distortions around difference, some of which we ourselves may be practicing. By and large within the women's movement today, white women focus upon their oppression as women and ignore differences of race, sexual preference, class, and age. There is a pretense to a homogeneity of experience covered by the word *sisterhood* that does not in fact exist.

Unacknowledged class differences rob women of each others' energy and creative insight. Recently a women's magazine collective made the decision for one issue to print only prose, saying poetry was a the less 'rigorous' or 'serious' art form. Yet even the form our creativity takes is often a class issue. Of all the art forms, poetry is the most economical. It is the one which is the most secret, which requires the least physical labor, the least material, and the one which can be done between shifts, in the hospital pantry, on the subway, and on scraps of surplus paper. Over the last few years, writing a novel on tight finances, I came to appreciate the enormous differences in the material demands between poetry and prose. As we reclaim our literature, poetry has been the major voice of poor, working class, and Colored women. A room of one's own may be a necessity for writing prose, but so are reams of paper, a typewriter, and plenty of time. The actual requirements to produce the visual arts also help determine, along class lines, whose art is whose. In this day of inflated prices for material, who are our sculptors, our painters, our photographers? When we speak of a broadly based women's culture, we need to be aware of the effect of class and economic differences on the supplies available for producing art.

As we move toward creating a society within which we can each flourish, ageism is another distortion of relationship which interferes with our vision.

By ignoring the past, we are encouraged to repeat its mistakes. The 'generation gap' is an important social tool for any repressive society. If the younger members of a community view the older members as contemptible or suspect or excess, they will never be able to join hands and examine the living memories of the community, nor ask the all-important question, 'Why?' This gives rise to a historical amnesia that keeps us working to invent the wheel every time we have to go to the store for bread.

We find ourselves having to repeat and relearn the same old lessons over and over that our mothers did because we do not pass on what we have learned, or because we are unable to listen. For instance, how many times has this all been said before? For another, who would have believed that once again our daughters are allowing their bodies to be hampered and purgatoried by girdles and high heels and hobble skirts?

Ignoring the differences of race between women and the implications of those differences presents the most serious threat to the mobilization of women's joint power.

As white women ignore their built-in privilege of whiteness and define *woman* in terms of their own experience alone, then women of Color become 'other,' the outsider whose experience and tradition is too 'alien' to comprehend. An example of this is the signal absence of the experience of women of Color as a resource for women's studies courses. The literature of women of Color is seldom included in women's literature courses and almost never in other literature courses, nor in women's studies as a whole. All too often, the excuse given is that the literatures of women of Color can only be taught by Colored women, or that they are too difficult to understand, or that classes cannot 'get into' them because they come out of experiences that are 'too different.' I have heard this argument presented by white women of otherwise quite clear intelligence, women who seem to have no trouble at all teaching and reviewing work that comes out of the vastly different experiences of Shakespeare, Molière, Dostoevsky, and Aristophanes. Surely there must be some other explanation.

This is a very complex question, but I believe one of the reasons white women have such difficulty reading Black women's work is because of their reluctance to see Black women as women and different from themselves. To examine Black women's literature effectively requires that we be seen as whole people in our actual complexities – as individuals, as women, as human – rather than as one of those problematic but familiar stereotypes provided in this society in place of genuine images of Black women. And I believe this holds true for the literatures of other women of Color who are not Black.

The literatures of all women of Color recreate the textures of our lives, and many white women are heavily invested in ignoring the real differences. For as long as any difference between us means one of us must be inferior, then the recognition of any difference must be fraught with guilt. To allow women of Color to step out of stereotypes is too guilt provoking, for it threatens the complacency of those women who view oppression only in terms of sex.

Refusing to recognize difference makes it impossible to see the different problems and pitfalls facing us as women.

Thus, in a patriarchal power system where white-skin privilege is a major prop, the entrapments used to neutralize Black women and white women are not the same. For example, it is easy for Black women to be used by the power structure against Black men, not because they are men, but because they are Black. Therefore, for Black women, it is necessary at all times to separate the needs of the oppressor from our own legitimate conflicts within our communities. This same problem does not exist for white women. Black women and men have shared racist oppression, we have developed joint defenses and joint vulnerabilities to each other that are not duplicated in the white community, with the exception of the relationship between Jewish women and Jewish men.

On the other hand, white women face the pitfall of being seduced into joining the oppressor under the pretense of sharing power. This possibility does not exist in the same way for women of Color. The tokenism that is sometimes extended to us is not an invitation to join power; our racial 'otherness' is a visible reality that makes that quite clear. For white women there is a wider range of pretended choices and rewards for identifying with patriarchal power and its tools.

Today, with the defeat of ERA, the tightening economy, and increased conservatism, it is easier once again for white women to believe the dangerous fantasy that if you are good enough, pretty enough, sweet enough, quiet enough, teach the children to behave, hate the right people, and marry the right men, then you will be allowed to co-exist with patriarchy in relative peace, at least until a man needs your job or the neighborhood rapist happens along. And true, unless one lives and loves in the trenches it is difficult to remember that the war against dehumanization is ceaseless.

But Black women and our children know the fabric of our lives is stitched with violence and with hatred, that there is no rest. We do not deal with it only on the picket lines, or in dark midnight alleys, or in the places where we dare to verbalize our resistance. For us, increasingly, violence weaves through the daily tissues of our living – in the supermarket, in the classroom, in the elevator, in the clinic and the schoolyard, from the plumber, the baker, the saleswoman, the bus driver, the bank teller, the waitress who does not serve us.

Some problems we share as women, some we do not. You fear your children will grow up to join the patriarchy and testify against you, we fear our children will be dragged from a car and shot down in the street, and you will turn your backs upon the reasons they are dying.

The threat of difference has been no less blinding to people of Color. Those of us who are Black must see that the reality of our lives and our struggle does not make us immune to the errors of ignoring and misnaming difference. Within Black communities where racism is a living reality, differences among us often seem dangerous and suspect. The need for unity is often misnamed as a need for homogeneity, and a Black feminist vision mistaken for betrayal of our common interests as a people. Because of the continuous battle against racial erasure that Black women and Black men share, some Black women still refuse to recognize that we are also oppressed as women, and that sexual hostility against Black women is practiced not only by the white racist society, but implemented within our Black communities as well. It is a disease striking the heart of Black nationhood, and silence will not make it disappear. Exacerbated by racism and the pressures of powerlessness, violence against Black women and children often becomes a standard within our communities, one by which manliness can be measured. But these woman-hating acts are rarely discussed as crimes against Black women.

As a group, women of Color are the lowest paid wage earners in america. We are the primary targets of abortion and sterilization abuse, here and abroad. In certain parts of Africa, small girls are still being sewed shut between their legs to keep them docile and for men's pleasure. This is known as female circumcision, and it is not a cultural affair as the late Jomo Kenyatta insisted, it is a crime against Black women.

Black women's literature is full of the pain of frequent assault, not only by a racist patriarchy, but also by Black men. Yet the necessity for and history of shared battle have made us, Black women, particularly vulnerable to the false accusation that anti-sexist is anti-Black. Meanwhile, womanhating as a recourse of the powerless is sapping strength from Black communities, and our very lives. Rape is on the increase, reported and unreported, and rape is not aggressive sexuality, it is sexualized aggression. As Kalamu ya Salaam, a Black male writer points out, 'As long as male domination exists, rape will exist. Only women revolting and men made conscious of their responsibility to fight sexism can collectively stop rape.'[2]

Differences between ourselves as Black women are also being misnamed and used to separate us from one another. As a Black lesbian feminist comfortable with the many different ingredients of my identity, and a woman committed to racial and sexual freedom from oppression, I find I am constantly being encouraged to pluck out some one aspect of myself and present this as the meaningful whole, eclipsing or denying the other parts of self. But this is a destructive and fragmenting way to live. My fullest concentration of energy is available to me only when I integrate all the parts of who I am, openly, allowing power from particular sources of my living to flow back and forth freely through all my different selves, without the restrictions of

2. From 'Rape: A Radical Analysis, An African-American Perspective' by Kalamu ya Salaam in *Black Books Bulletin*, vol. 6, no. 4 (1980).

externally imposed definition. Only then can I bring myself and my energies as a whole to the service of those struggles which I embrace as part of my living.

A fear of lesbians, or of being accused of being a lesbian, has led many Black women into testifying against themselves. It has led some of us into destructive alliances, and others into despair and isolation. In the white women's communities, heterosexism is sometimes a result of identifying with the white patriarchy, a rejection of that interdependence between women-identified women which allows the self to be, rather than to be used in the service of men. Sometimes it reflects a die-hard belief in the protective coloration of heterosexual relationships, sometimes a self-hate which all women have to fight against, taught us from birth.

Although elements of these attitudes exist for all women, there are particular resonances of heterosexism and homophobia among Black women. Despite the fact that woman-bonding has a long and honorable history in the African and African-american communities, and despite the knowledge and accomplishments of many strong and creative women-identified Black women in the political, social and cultural fields, heterosexual Black women often tend to ignore or discount the existence and work of Black lesbians. Part of this attitude has come from an understandable terror of Black male attack within the close confines of Black society, where the punishment for any female self-assertion is still to be accused of being a lesbian and therefore unworthy of the attention or support of the scarce Black male. But part of this need to misname and ignore Black lesbians comes from a very real fear that openly women-identified Black women who are no longer dependent upon men for their self-definition may well reorder our whole concept of social relationships.

Black women who once insisted that lesbianism was a white woman's problem now insist that Black lesbians are a threat to Black nationhood, are consorting with the enemy, are basically un-Black. These accusations, coming from the very women to whom we look for deep and real understanding, have served to keep many Black lesbians in hiding, caught between the racism of white women and the homophobia of their sisters. Often, their work has been ignored, trivialized, or misnamed, as with the work of Angelina Grimke, Alice Dunbar-Nelson, Lorraine Hansberry. Yet women-bonded women have always been some part of the power of Black communities, from our unmarried aunts to the amazons of Dahomey.

And it is certainly not Black lesbians who are

assaulting women and raping children and grand-
mothers on the streets of our communities.

Across this country, as in Boston during the spring
of 1979 following the unsolved murders of twelve
Black women, Black lesbians are spearheading move-
ments against violence against Black women.

What are the particular details within each of our
lives that can be scrutinized and altered to help
bring about change? How do we redefine difference
for all women? It is not our differences which separate women, but our reluctance to recognize those
differences and to deal effectively with the distortions which have resulted from the ignoring and
misnaming of those differences.

As a tool of social control, women have been
encouraged to recognize only one area of human difference as legitimate, those differences which exist
between women and men. And we have learned to
deal across those differences with the urgency of all
oppressed subordinates. All of us have had to learn
to live or work or co-exist with men, from our fathers
on. We have recognized and negotiated these differences, even when this recognition only continued
the old dominant/subordinate mode of human relationship, where the oppressed must recognize the
masters' difference in order to survive.

But our future survival is predicated upon our

ability to relate within equality. As women, we must root out internalized patterns of oppression within ourselves if we are to move beyond the most superficial aspects of social change. Now we must recognize differences among women who are our equals, neither inferior nor superior, and devise ways to use each others' difference to enrich our visions and our joint struggles.

The future of our earth may depend upon the ability of all women to identify and develop new definitions of power and new patterns of relating across difference. The old definitions have not served us, nor the earth that supports us. The old patterns, no matter how cleverly rearranged to imitate progress, still condemn us to cosmetically altered repetitions of the same old exchanges, the same old guilt, hatred, recrimination, lamentation, and suspicion.

For we have, built into all of us, old blueprints of expectation and response, old structures of oppression, and these must be altered at the same time as we alter the living conditions which are a result of those structures. *For the master's tools will never dismantle the master's house.*

As Paulo Freire shows so well in *The Pedagogy of the Oppressed*,[3] the true focus of revolutionary

3. Seabury Press, New York, 1970.

change is never merely the oppressive situations which we seek to escape, but that piece of the oppressor which is planted deep within each of us, and which knows only the oppressors' tactics, the oppressors' relationships.

Change means growth, and growth can be painful. But we sharpen self-definition by exposing the self in work and struggle together with those whom we define as different from ourselves, although sharing the same goals. For Black and white, old and young, lesbian and heterosexual women alike, this can mean new paths to our survival.

> We have chosen each other
> and the edge of each others' battles
> the war is the same
> if we lose
> someday women's blood will congeal
> upon a dead planet
> if we win
> there is no telling
> we seek beyond history
> for a new and more possible meeting.[4]

4. From 'Outlines,' unpublished poem.

Scratching the Surface: Some Notes on Barriers to Women and Loving[1]

Racism: The belief in the inherent superiority of one race over all others and thereby the right to dominance.

Sexism: The belief in the inherent superiority of one sex and thereby the right to dominance.

Heterosexism: The belief in the inherent superiority of one pattern of loving and thereby its right to dominance.

Homophobia: The fear of feelings of love for members of one's own sex and therefore the hatred of those feelings in others.

The above forms of human blindness stem from the same root – an inability to recognize the notion of difference as a dynamic human force, one which is enriching rather than threatening to the defined self, when there are shared goals.

1. First published in *The Black Scholar*, vol. 9, no. 7 (1978).

To a large degree, at least verbally, the Black community has moved beyond the 'two steps behind her man' concept of sexual relations sometimes mouthed as desirable during the sixties. This was a time when the myth of the Black matriarchy as a social disease was being presented by racist forces to redirect our attentions away from the real sources of Black oppression.

For Black women as well as Black men, it is axiomatic that if we do not define ourselves for ourselves, we will be defined by others – for their use and to our detriment. The development of self-defined Black women, ready to explore and pursue our power and interests within our communities, is a vital component in the war for Black liberation. The image of the Angolan woman with a baby on one arm and a gun in the other is neither romantic nor fanciful. When Black women in this country come together to examine our sources of strength and support, and to recognize our common social, cultural, emotional, and political interests, it is a development which can only contribute to the power of the Black community as a whole. It can certainly never diminish it. For it is through the coming together of self-actualized individuals, female and male, that any real advances can be made. The old sexual power relationships based on a dominant/subordinate model between unequals have not served us as a people, nor as individuals.

Black women who define ourselves and our goals beyond the sphere of a sexual relationship can bring to any endeavor the realized focus of completed and therefore empowered individuals. Black women and Black men who recognize that the development of their particular strengths and interests does not diminish the other do not need to diffuse their energies fighting for control over each other. We can focus our attentions against the real economic, political, and social forces at the heart of this society which are ripping us and our children and our worlds apart.

Increasingly, despite opposition, Black women are coming together to explore and to alter those manifestations of our society which oppress us in different ways from those that oppress Black men. This is no threat to Black men. It is only seen as one by those Black men who choose to embody within themselves those same manifestations of female oppression. For instance, no Black man has ever been forced to bear a child he did not want or could not support. Enforced sterilization and unavailable abortions are tools of oppression against Black women, as is rape. Only to those Black men who are unclear about the pathways of their own definition can the self-actualization and self-protective bonding of Black women be seen as a threatening development.

Today, the red herring of lesbian-baiting is being used in the Black community to obscure the true face of racism/sexism. Black women sharing close ties with each other, politically or emotionally, are not the enemies of Black men. Too frequently, however, some Black men attempt to rule by fear those Black women who are more ally than enemy. These tactics are expressed as threats of emotional rejection: 'Their poetry wasn't too bad but I couldn't take all those lezzies.' The Black man saying this is code-warning every Black woman present interested in a relationship with a man – and most Black women are – that (1) if she wishes to have her work considered by him she must eschew any other allegiance except to him and (2) any woman who wishes to retain his friendship and/or support had better not be 'tainted' by woman-identified interests.

If such threats of labeling, vilification and/or emotional isolation are not enough to bring Black women docilely into camp as followers, or persuade us to avoid each other politically and emotionally, then the rule by terror can be expressed physically, as on the campus of a New York State college in the late 1970s, where Black women sought to come together around women's concerns. Phone calls threatening violence were made to those Black women who dared to explore the possibilities of a feminist connection with non-Black women. Some of these women, intimidated by threats and the withdrawal of Black male approval, did turn against their sisters. When threats did not prevent the attempted coalition of feminists, the resulting campus-wide hysteria left some Black women beaten and raped. Whether the threats by Black men actually led to these assaults, or merely encouraged the climate of hostility within which they could occur, the results upon the women attacked were the same.

War, imprisonment, and 'the street' have decimated the ranks of Black males of marriageable age. The fury of many Black heterosexual women against white women who date Black men is rooted in this unequal sexual equation within the Black community, since whatever threatens to widen that equation is deeply and articulately resented. But this is essentially unconstructive resentment because it extends sideways only. It can never result in true progress on the issue because it does not question the vertical lines of power or authority, nor the sexist assumptions which dictate the terms of that competition. And the racism of white women might be better addressed where it is less complicated by their own sexual oppression. In this situation it is not the non-Black woman who calls the tune, but rather the Black man who turns away from himself in his sisters or who, through a fear borrowed from white men, reads her strength not as a resource but as a challenge.

All too often the message comes loud and clear to Black women from Black men; 'I am the only prize worth having and there are not too many of me, and remember, I can always go elsewhere. So if you want me, you'd better stay in your place which is away from one another, or I will call you "lesbian" and wipe you out.' Black women are programmed to define ourselves within this male attention and to compete with each other for it rather than to recognize and move upon our common interests.

The tactic of encouraging horizontal hostility to becloud more pressing issues of oppression is by no means new, nor limited to relations between women. The same tactic is used to encourage separation between Black women and Black men. In discussions around the hiring and firing of Black faculty at universities, the charge is frequently heard that Black women are more easily hired than are Black men. For this reason, Black women's problems of promotion and tenure are not to be considered important since they are only 'taking jobs away from Black men.' Here again, energy is being wasted on fighting each other over the pitifully few crumbs allowed us rather than being used, in a joining of forces, to fight for a more realistic ratio of Black faculty. The latter would be a vertical battle against racist policies of the academic structure itself, one which could result in real power and change. It is the structure at the top which desires changelessness and which profits from these apparently endless kitchen wars.

Instead of keeping our attentions focused upon our real needs, enormous energy is being wasted in the Black community today in antilesbian hysteria. Yet women-identified women – those who sought their own destinies and attempted to execute them in the absence of male support – have been around in all of our communities for a long time. As Yvonne Flowers of York College pointed out in a recent discussion, the unmarried aunt, childless or otherwise, whose home and resources were often a welcome haven for different members of the family, was a familiar figure in many of our childhoods. And within the homes of our Black communities today, it is not the Black lesbian who is battering and raping our underage girl-children out of displaced and sickening frustration.

The Black lesbian has come under increasing attack from both Black men and heterosexual Black women. In the same way that the existence of the self-defined Black woman is no threat to the self-defined Black man, the Black lesbian is an emotional threat only to those Black women who are problematic in some way. For so long, we have been encouraged to view each other with suspicion, as eternal competitors, or as the visible face of our own self-rejection.

Yet traditionally, Black women have always bonded together in support of each other, however uneasily and in the face of whatever other allegiances which militated against that bonding. We have banded together with each other for wisdom and strength and support, even when it was only in relationship to one man. We need only look at the close, although highly complex and involved, relationship between African co-wives, or at the Amazon warriors of ancient Dahomey who fought together as the King's main and most ferocious bodyguard. We need only look at the more promising power wielded by the West African Market Women Associations of today, and those governments which have risen and fallen at their pleasure.

In a retelling of her life, a ninety-two-year-old Efik-Ibibio woman of Nigeria recalls her love for another woman:

I had a woman friend to whom I revealed my secrets. She was very fond of keeping secrets to herself. We acted as husband and wife. We always moved hand in glove and my husband and hers knew about our relationship. The villagers nick-named us twin sisters. When I was out of gear with my husband, she would be the one to restore peace. I often sent my children to go and work for her in return for her kindnesses to me. My hus-band being more fortunate to get more pieces of land than her husband, allowed some to her, even though she was not my co-wife.[2]

On the West Coast of Africa, the Fon of Dahomey still have twelve different kinds of marriage. One of them is known as 'giving the goat to the buck,' where a woman of independent means marries another woman who then may or may not bear chil-dren, all of whom will belong to the blood line of the first woman. Some marriages of this kind are arranged to provide heirs for women of means who wish to remain 'free,' and some are lesbian relationships. Marriages like these occur throughout Africa, in several different places among different

2. Iris Andreski, *Old Wives Tales: Life-Stories of African Women* (Schocken Books, New York, 1970), p. 131.

peoples.[3] Routinely, the women involved are accepted members of their communities, evaluated not by their sexuality but by their respective places within the community.

While a piece of each Black woman remembers the old ways of another place – when we enjoyed each other in a sisterhood of work and play and power – other pieces of us, less functional, eye one another with suspicion. In the interests of separation, Black women have been taught to view each other as always suspect, heartless competitors for the scarce male, the all-important prize that could legitimize our existence. This dehumanizing denial of self is no less lethal than the dehumanization of racism to which it is so closely allied.

If the recent attack upon lesbians in the Black community is based solely upon an aversion to the idea of sexual contact between members of the same sex (a contact which has existed for ages in most of the female compounds across the African continent), why then is the idea of sexual contact between Black men so much more easily accepted, or unremarked? Is the imagined threat simply the existence

3. Melville Herskovits, *Dahomey,* 2 vols. (Northwestern University Press, Evanston, Illinois, 1967), 1: 320 – 322.

of a self-motivated, self-defined Black woman who will not fear nor suffer terrible retribution from the gods because she does not necessarily seek her face in a man's eyes, even if he has fathered her children? Female-headed households in the Black community are not always situations by default.

The distortion of relationship which says 'I disagree with you, so I must destroy you' leaves us as Black people with basically uncreative victories, defeated in any common struggle. This jugular vein psychology is based on the fallacy that your assertion or affirmation of self is an attack upon my self – or that my defining myself will somehow prevent or retard your self-definition. The supposition that one sex needs the other's acquiescence in order to exist prevents both from moving together as self-defined persons toward a common goal.

This kind of action is a prevalent error among oppressed peoples. It is based upon the false notion that there is only a limited and particular amount of freedom that must be divided up between us, with the largest and juiciest pieces of liberty going as spoils to the victor or the stronger. So instead of joining together to fight for more, we quarrel between ourselves for a larger slice of the one pie. Black women fight between ourselves over men, instead of pursuing and using who we are and our strengths for lasting change; Black women and men fight between ourselves over who has more of a right to freedom, instead of seeing each other's struggle as part of our own and vital to our common goals; Black and white women fight between ourselves over who is the more oppressed, instead of seeing those areas in which our causes are the same. (Of course, this last separation is worsened by the intransigent racism that white women too often fail to, or cannot, address in themselves.)

At a recent Black literary conference, a heterosexual Black woman stated that to endorse lesbianism was to endorse the death of our race. This position reflects acute fright or a faulty reasoning, for once again it ascribes false power to difference. To the racist, Black people are so powerful that the presence of one can contaminate a whole lineage; to the heterosexist, lesbians are so powerful that the presence of one can contaminate the whole sex. This position supposes that if we do not eradicate lesbianism in the Black community, all Black women will become lesbians. It also supposes that lesbians do not have children. Both suppositions are patently false.

As Black women, we must deal with all the realities of our lives which place us at risk as Black women – homosexual or heterosexual. In 1977 in Detroit, a young Black actress, Patricia Cowan, was invited to audition for a play called *Hammer* and was then hammered to death by the young Black male playwright. Patricia Cowan was not killed because she was Black. She was killed because she was a Black woman, and her cause belongs to us all. History does not record whether or not she was a lesbian, but only that she had a four-year-old child.

Of the four groups, Black and white women, Black and white men, Black women have the lowest average wage. This is a vital concern for us all, no matter with whom we sleep.

As Black women we have the right and responsibility to define ourselves and to seek our allies in common cause: with Black men against racism, and with each other and white women against sexism. But most of all, as Black women we have the right and responsibility to recognize each other without fear and to love where we choose. Both lesbian and heterosexual Black women today share a history of bonding and strength to which our sexual identities and our other differences must not blind us.

Poetry Is Not a Luxury[1]

The quality of light by which we scrutinize our lives has direct bearing upon the product which we live, and upon the changes which we hope to bring about through those lives. It is within this light that we form those ideas by which we pursue our magic and make it realized. This is poetry as illumination, for it is through poetry that we give name to those ideas which are – until the poem – nameless and formless, about to be birthed, but already felt. That distillation of experience from which true poetry springs births thought as dream births concept, as feeling births idea, as knowledge births (precedes) understanding.

As we learn to bear the intimacy of scrutiny and to flourish within it, as we learn to use the products of that scrutiny for power within our living, those fears which rule our lives and form our silences begin to lose their control over us.

1. First published in *Chrysalis: A Magazine of Female Culture*, no. 3 (1977).

For each of us as women, there is a dark place within, where hidden and growing our true spirit rises, 'beautiful/ and tough as chestnut/ stanchions against (y)our nightmare of weakness/[2] and of impotence.'

These places of possibility within ourselves are dark because they are ancient and hidden; they have survived and grown strong through that darkness. Within these deep places, each one of us holds an incredible reserve of creativity and power, of unexamined and unrecorded emotion and feeling. The woman's place of power within each one of us is neither white nor surface; it is dark, it is ancient, and it is deep.

When we view living in the european mode only as a problem to be solved, we rely solely upon our ideas to make us free, for these were what the white fathers told us were precious.

But as we come more into touch with our own ancient, noneuropean consciousness of living as a situation to be experienced and interacted with, we learn more and more to cherish our feelings, and to respect those hidden sources of our power from where true knowledge and, therefore, lasting action comes.

At this point in time, I believe that women carry

2. From 'Black Mother Woman,' first published in *From A Land Where Other People Live* (Broadside Press, Detroit, 1973), and collected in *Chosen Poems: Old and New* (W.W. Norton and Company, New York, 1982) p. 53.

within ourselves the possibility for fusion of these two approaches so necessary for survival, and we come closest to this combination in our poetry. I speak here of poetry as a revelatory distillation of experience, not the sterile word play that, too often, the white fathers distorted the word *poetry* to mean – in order to cover a desperate wish for imagination without insight.

For women, then, poetry is not a luxury. It is a vital necessity of our existence. It forms the quality of the light within which we predicate our hopes and dreams toward survival and change, first made into language, then into idea, then into more tangible action. Poetry is the way we help give name to the nameless so it can be thought. The farthest horizons of our hopes and fears are cobbled by our poems, carved from the rock experiences of our daily lives.

As they become known to and accepted by us, our feelings and the honest exploration of them become sanctuaries and spawning grounds for the most radical and daring of ideas. They become a safe-house for that difference so necessary to change and the conceptualization of any meaningful action. Right now, I could name at least ten ideas I would have found intolerable or incomprehensible and frightening, except as they came after dreams and poems. This is not idle fantasy, but a disciplined attention to the true

meaning of 'it feels right to me.' We can train ourselves to respect our feelings and to transpose them
into a language so they can be shared. And where that
language does not yet exist, it is our poetry which
helps to fashion it. Poetry is not only dream and
vision: it is the skeleton architecture of our lives. It
lays the foundations for a future of change, a bridge
across our fears of what has never been before.

Possibility is neither forever nor instant. It is not
easy to sustain belief in its efficacy. We can sometimes
work long and hard to establish one beachhead of real
resistance to the deaths we are expected to live, only
to have that beachhead assaulted or threatened
by those canards we have been socialized to fear,
or by the withdrawal of those approvals that we
have been warned to seek for safety. Women see ourselves diminished or softened by the falsely benign
accusations of childishness, of nonuniversality, of
changeability, of sensuality. And who asks the question: Am I altering your aura, your ideas, your dreams,
or am I merely moving you to temporary and reactive
action? And even though the latter is no mean task, it
is one that must be seen within the context of a need
for true alteration of the very foundations of our lives.

The white fathers told us: I think, therefore I am.
The Black mother within each of us – the poet –
whispers in our dreams: I feel, therefore I can be

free. Poetry coins the language to express and charter this revolutionary demand, the implementation of that freedom.

However, experience has taught us that action in the now is also necessary, always. Our children cannot dream unless they live, they cannot live unless they are nourished, and who else will feed them the real food without which their dreams will be no different from ours? If you want us to change the world someday, we at least have to live long enough to grow up! shouts the child.

Sometimes we drug ourselves with dreams of new ideas. The head will save us. The brain alone will set us free. But there are no new ideas still waiting in the wings to save us as women, as human. There are only old and forgotten ones, new combinations, extrapolations and recognitions from within ourselves – along with the renewed courage to try them out. And we must constantly encourage ourselves and each other to attempt the heretical actions that our dreams imply, and so many of our old ideas disparage. In the forefront of our move toward change, there is only poetry to hint at possibility made real. Our poems formulate the implications of ourselves, what we feel within and dare make real (or bring action into accordance with), our fears, our hopes, our most cherished terrors.

For within living structures defined by profit, by linear power, by institutional dehumanization, our feelings were not meant to survive. Kept around as unavoidable adjuncts or pleasant pastimes, feelings were expected to kneel to thought as women were expected to kneel to men. But women have survived. As poets. And there are no new pains. We have felt them all already. We have hidden that fact in the same place where we have hidden our power. They surface in our dreams, and it is our dreams that point the way to freedom. Those dreams are made realizable through our poems that give us the strength and courage to see, to feel, to speak, and to dare.

If what we need to dream, to move our spirits most deeply and directly toward and through promise, is discounted as a luxury, then we give up the core – the fountain – of our power, our womanness; we give up the future of our worlds.

For there are no new ideas. There are only new ways of making them felt – of examining what those ideas feel like being lived on Sunday morning at 7 A.M., after brunch, during wild love, making war, giving birth, mourning our dead – while we suffer the old longings, battle the old warnings and fears of being silent and impotent and alone, while we taste new possibilities and strengths.

Uses of the Erotic

There are many kinds of power, used and unused, acknowledged or otherwise. The erotic is a resource within each of us that lies in a deeply female and spiritual plane, firmly rooted in the power of our unexpressed or unrecognized feeling. In order to perpetuate itself, every oppression must corrupt or distort those various sources of power within the culture of the oppressed that can provide energy for change. For women, this has meant a suppression of the erotic as a considered source of power and information within our lives.

We have been taught to suspect this resource, vilified, abused, and devalued within western society. On the one hand, the superficially erotic has been encouraged as a sign of female inferiority; on the other hand, women have been made to suffer and to feel both contemptible and suspect by virtue of its existence.

It is a short step from there to the false belief that only by the suppression of the erotic within our lives and consciousness can women be truly strong. But that strength is illusory, for it is fashioned within the context of male models of power.

As women, we have come to distrust that power which rises from our deepest and non-rational knowledge. We have been warned against it all our lives by the male world, which values this depth of feeling enough to keep women around in order to exercise it in the service of men, but which fears this same depth too much to examine the possibilities of it within themselves. So women are maintained at a distant/inferior position to be psychically milked, much the same way ants maintain colonies of aphids to provide a life-giving substance for their masters.

But the erotic offers a well of replenishing and provocative force to the woman who does not fear its revelation, nor succumb to the belief that sensation is enough.

The erotic has often been misnamed by men and used against women. It has been made into the confused, the trivial, the psychotic, the plasticized sensation. For this reason, we have often turned away from the exploration and consideration of the erotic as a source of power and information, confusing it with its opposite, the pornographic. But pornography is a direct denial of the power of the erotic, for it represents the suppression of true feeling. Pornography emphasizes sensation without feeling.

The erotic is a measure between the beginnings of our sense of self and the chaos of our strongest feelings. It is an internal sense of satisfaction to which, once we have experienced it, we know we can aspire. For having experienced the fullness of this depth of feeling and recognizing its power, in honour and self-respect we can require no less of ourselves.

It is never easy to demand the most from ourselves, from our lives, from our work. To encourage excellence is to go beyond the encouraged mediocrity of our society. But giving in to the fear of feeling and working to capacity is a luxury only the unintentional can afford, and the unintentional are those who do not wish to guide their own destinies.

This internal requirement towards excellence which we learn from the erotic must not be misconstrued as demanding the impossible from ourselves nor from others. Such a demand incapacitates everyone in the process. For the erotic is not a question only of what we do; it is a question of how acutely and fully we can feel in the doing. Once we know the extent to which we are capable of feeling that sense of satisfaction and completion, we can then observe which of our various life endeavours bring us closest to that fullness.

The aim of each thing which we do is to make our lives and the lives of our children richer and more possible. Within the celebration of the erotic in all our endeavours, my work becomes a conscious decision – a longed-for bed which I enter gratefully and from which I rise up empowered.

Of course, women so empowered are dangerous. So we are taught to separate the erotic demand from most vital areas of our lives other than sex. And the lack of concern for the erotic root and satisfactions of our work is felt in our disaffection from so much of what we do. For instance, how often do we truly love our work even at its most difficult?

The principal horror of any system which defines the good in terms of profit rather than in terms of human need, or which defines human need to the exclusion of the psychic and emotional components of that need – the principal horror of such a system is that it robs our work of its erotic value, its erotic power and life appeal and fulfilment. Such a system reduces work to a travesty of necessities, a duty by which we earn bread or oblivion for ourselves and those we love. But this is tantamount to blinding a painter and then telling her to improve her work, and to enjoy the act of painting. It is not only next to impossible, it is also profoundly cruel.

As women, we need to examine the ways in which our world can be truly different. I am speaking here of the necessity for reassessing the quality of all the aspects of our lives and of our work, and of how we move towards and through them.

The very word *erotic* comes from the Greek word *eros*, the personification of love in all its aspects – born of Chaos, and personifying creative power and harmony. When I speak of the erotic, then, I speak of it as an assertion of the lifeforce of women; of that creative energy empowered, the knowledge and use of which we are now reclaiming in our language, our history, our dancing, our loving, our work, our lives.

There are frequent attempts to equate pornography and eroticism, two diametrically opposed uses of the sexual. Because of these attempts, it has become fashionable to separate the spiritual (psychic and emotional) from the political, to see them as contradictory or antithetical. 'What do you mean, a poetic revolutionary, a meditating gunrunner?' In the same way, we have attempted to separate the spiritual and the erotic, thereby reducing the spiritual to a world of flattened affect, a world of the ascetic who aspires to feel nothing. But nothing is farther from the truth. For the ascetic position is one of the highest fear, the gravest immobility. The severe abstinence of the ascetic becomes the ruling obsession. And it is one not of self-discipline but of self-abnegation.

The dichotomy between the spiritual and the political is also false, resulting from an incomplete attention to our erotic knowledge. For the bridge which connects them is formed by the erotic – the sensual – those physical, emotional, and psychic expressions of what is deepest and strongest and richest within each of us, being shared: the passions of love, in its deepest meanings.

Beyond the superficial, the considered phrase 'It feels right to me' acknowledges the strength of the erotic into a true knowledge, for what that means is the first and most powerful guiding light towards any understanding. And understanding is a handmaiden which can only wait upon, or clarify, that knowledge, deeply born. The erotic is the nurturer or nursemaid of all our deepest knowledge.

The erotic functions for me in several ways, and the first is in providing the power which comes from sharing deeply any pursuit with another person. The sharing of joy, whether physical, emotional, psychic, or intellectual, forms a bridge between the sharers which can be the basis for understanding much of what is not shared between them, and lessens the threat of their difference.

Another important way in which the erotic connection functions is the open and fearless underlining of my capacity for joy. In the way my body stretches to music and opens into response, hearkening to its deepest rhythms, so every level upon which I sense also opens to the erotically satisfying experience, whether it is dancing, building a bookcase, writing a poem, examining an idea.

That self-connection shared is a measure of the joy which I know myself to be capable of feeling, a reminder of my capacity for feeling. And that deep and irreplaceable knowledge of my capacity for joy comes to demand from all of my life that it be lived within the knowledge that such satisfaction is possible, and does not have to be called *marriage*, nor *god*, nor an *afterlife*.

This is one reason why the erotic is so feared, and so often relegated to the bedroom alone, when it is recognized at all. For once we begin to feel deeply all the aspects of our lives, we begin to demand from ourselves and from our life-pursuits that they feel in accordance with that joy which we know ourselves to be capable of. Our erotic knowledge empowers us, becomes a lens through which we scrutinize all aspects of our existence, forcing us to evaluate those aspects honestly in terms of their relative meaning within our lives. And this is a grave responsibility, projected from within each of us, not to settle for the convenient, the shoddy, the conventionally expected, nor the merely safe.

During World War Two, we bought sealed plastic packets of white, uncoloured margarine, with a tiny, intense pellet of yellow colouring perched like a topa just inside the clear skin of the bag. We would leave the margarine out for a while to soften, and then we would pinch the little pellet to break it inside the bag, releasing the rich yellowness into the soft pale mass of margarine. Then taking it carefully between our fingers, we would knead it gently back and forth, over and over, until the colour had spread throughout the whole pound bag of margarine, thoroughly colouring it.

I find the erotic such a kernel within myself. When released from its intense and constrained pellet, it flows through and colours my life with a kind of energy that heightens and sensitizes and strengthens all my experience.

We have been raised to fear the yes within ourselves, our deepest cravings. But, once recognized, those which do not enhance our future lose their power and can be altered. The fear of our desires keeps them suspect and indiscriminately powerful, for to suppress any truth is to give it strength beyond endurance. The fear that we cannot grow beyond whatever distortions we may find within ourselves keeps us docile and loyal and obedient, externally defined, and leads us to accept many facets of our oppression as women.

When we live outside ourselves, and by that I mean on external directives only rather than from our internal knowledge and needs, when we live away from those erotic guides from within ourselves, then our lives are limited by external and alien forms, and we conform to the needs of a structure that is not based on human need, let alone an individual's. But when we begin to live from within outward, in touch with the power of the erotic within ourselves, and allowing that power to inform and illuminate our actions upon the world around us, then we begin to be responsible to ourselves in the deepest sense. For as we begin to recognize our deepest feelings, we begin to give up, of necessity, being satisfied with suffering and self-negation, and with the numbness which so often seems like their only alternative in our society. Our acts against oppression become integral with self, motivated and empowered from within.

In touch with the erotic, I become less willing to accept powerlessness, or those other supplied states of being which are not native to me, such as resignation, despair, self-effacement, depression, self-denial.

And yes, there is a hierarchy. There is a difference between painting a back fence and writing a poem, but only one of quantity. And there is, for me, no difference between writing a good poem and moving into sunlight against the body of a woman I love.

This brings me to the last consideration of the erotic. To share the power of each other's feelings is different from using another's feelings as we would use a Kleenex. When we look the other way from our experience, erotic or otherwise, we use rather than share the feelings of those others who participate in the experience with us. And use without consent of the used is abuse.

In order to be utilized, our erotic feelings must be recognized. The need for sharing deep feeling is a human need. But within the european-american tradition, this need is satisfied by certain proscribed erotic comings-together. These occasions are almost always characterized by a simultaneous looking away, a pretence of calling them something else, whether a religion, a fit, mob violence, or even playing doctor. And this misnaming of the need and the deed give rise to that distortion which results in pornography and obscenity – the abuse of feeling.

When we look away from the importance of the

erotic in the development and sustenance of our power, or when we look away from ourselves as we satisfy our erotic needs in concert with others, we use each other as objects of satisfaction rather than share our joy in the satisfying, rather than make connection with our similarities and our differences. To refuse to be conscious of what we are feeling at any time, however comfortable that might seem, is to deny a large part of the experience, and to allow ourselves to be reduced to the pornographic, the abused, and the absurd.

The erotic cannot be felt secondhand. As a Black lesbian feminist, I have a particular feeling, knowledge, and understanding for those sisters with whom I have danced hard, played, or even fought. This deep participation has often been the forerunner for joint concerted actions not possible before.

But this erotic charge is not easily shared by women who continue to operate under an exclusively european-american male tradition. I know it was not available to me when I was trying to adapt my consciousness to this mode of living and sensation.

Only now, I find more and more women-identified women brave enough to risk sharing the erotic's electrical charge without having to look away, and without distorting the enormously powerful and creative nature of that exchange. Recognizing the power of the erotic within our lives can give us the energy to pursue genuine change within our world, rather than merely settling for a shift of characters in the same weary drama.

For not only do we touch our most profoundly creative source, but we do that which is female and self-affirming in the face of a racist, patriarchal, and anti-erotic society.